Caring
Is
Living

Hints of Explanations

by
Dale Francis

The Thomas More Press
Chicago, Illinois

Contents

Along with biographical information, the editors of a reference book wanted an answer to a question. What, they asked, have been the primary influences in your life, to what do you attribute your achievements, what has most influenced your life?

I wrote in response to this question—

Two things have directed my life. My belief in God and my conviction that believing in God compels me to care about people.

And that's the truth.

FOREWORD

When Thomas More Press editor Joel Wells wrote to me about a book he thought I might write, he said, "I'm sure you'd agree that people need all the help they can get today simply to lead decent, Christian lives, especially in the face of suffering, marital, physical and emotional problems and stresses. We're hoping that you might draw upon your experience as well as those of the many whom you have helped and counseled or simply come in contact with in order to write a book that would offer Christian inspiration growing out of real life."

I did a lot of thinking about what Joel suggested I might do. One thing I knew was that I couldn't and wouldn't write one of those books that tell you how to meet and solve your problems. I wasn't certain I could write the kind of book he wanted at all.

People do bring their burdens to me. For some reason that has been true all my life. I think it is probably because I do listen to people, because I do care about people. It certainly isn't because I can solve their problems for them or lift the burdens from them.

I never did feel comfortable offering people advice and the older I get the less comfortable I am. We are all so completely individuals. The burdens we must bear and the problems we must face are uniquely our own. So I distrust facile solutions that suggest all you need do is adopt a certain philosophy of life and all of your problems will be solved.

But there is something I do believe. I believe that in sharing experiences we can help each other. I've discovered that when someone comes to me with a burden or a problem, I can say that while I'm not certain what he should do, I could tell him how it was with me when I faced a similar problem or what it was someone I knew did while carrying the same kind of burden.

When I've done this I've discovered that while my own experiences or the experiences of others might not offer an answer, there might be a hint of an explanation of something that might help.

What I have tried to do in this book is simply to offer a sharing of myself, of things I've experienced, of things I've learned that have had meaning in my life, of people I've known whose lives have inspired me. It is my hope that somewhere in the opening of myself to you there will be times you gain some hints of explanations for yourself, that you'll think, "There's something that might help me."

I come into contact with people and their problems more today than ever before in my life, probably more than most people do. People write to me of the problems they face, the burdens they bear, not as they would write to an advice columnist, but simply to have someone to share their concern with them.

Most of these letters come through "Powerhouse," a prayer group made up, for the most part, of *Our Sunday Visitor* readers. We pray for each other. In the last

two years I have received more than 10,000 letters from
some of the most wonderful people in the world. They
share with me the crosses they bear, the problems they
face. It is not because they think I can offer them solutions. In a very real sense, they just leave their burdens
with me. The idea of Powerhouse is that we should
care about others, pray for others, turn away from
concern for ourselves to concern for others, to allow
others to pray for us as we pray for them.

I read every one of those letters, allow no one else to
read them, for I accept them as the confidences they
are. In the monthly letter I write to the members of
Powerhouse, I do not quote directly from or identify
those who have written to me, again because what has
been written to me I consider to be in confidence, but I
do pass on to all the members the kinds of burdens
others face.

In this book I have often prefaced my own sharing
of experiences with some of the problems I know,
through letters I've received, to be burdening people.
The prefaces are not direct quotations but a kind of
summing up of many letters.

I said the letters I receive come from some of the
most wonderful people in the world. That is true. I am
given the blessing of knowing in a special way the
courage and faith of thousands of people.

The letters I receive sometimes almost literally tear
me apart. So many people carry such great burdens.
Some people write to me only once but hundreds write
continuing letters, sharing with me the way things are

going in their families. Sometimes happy solutions are found, sometimes what have seemed to be problems that could be solved become great tragedies.

But if I am torn apart by the letters I receive, I am also edified by most of them. It is rare, almost so rare it never happens, that the people who write to me are feeling sorry for themselves. They are ordinary people, facing extraordinary problems, with courage and with faith.

We are all people with burdens and with problems. But we are not alone. We are not alone because we can seek strength from God, who never abandons us. But in another sense we are not alone—we are not alone because we are united as a people, all of us with burdens we must bear, all of us with problems we must face.

We must care about each other and in the caring there is a sharing in which we can offer our strengths and weaknesses to each other and in the sharing we may find hints of explanations in each other's lives.

CHAPTER 1
That's Really Living

There's a story they tell in Texas about this multi-millionaire who planned his own burial. He arranged that when he died he would be buried in an $850 silk suit, $350 alligator boots on his feet, a $150 Stetson on his head, a $5 Havana cigar clamped between his teeth, sitting behind the wheel of a brand-new pink Cadillac.

So, as Time used to say it must to all men, death came to this multi-millionaire and the burial arrangements were made just as he had planned them.

When the services were over and the friends and relatives had gone, the final tasks were left to a crew of workers. As the big car was lowered into the grave, one of the workers leaned over, peered into the window for one last look at the deceased.

He saw him there in his $850 silk suit, $350 alligator boots on his feet, a $150 Stetson on his head, a $5 Havana cigar clamped between his teeth, sitting behind the wheel of the brand-new pink Cadillac, and he sighed and said, "Man, that's really living."

That's a joke but the joke isn't just about a man physically dead going to the grave with luxurious possessions. The real joke is on those who think that possessions really constitute living.

Really living isn't in the gathering of things; really living isn't in what we possess but what we give away. Really living isn't in what we are able to do for ourselves but what we are able to do for others.

When we center our thoughts and our actions on ourselves then we can die without ever having lived. It is only when we reach out beyond ourselves to others, only when we expand our consciousness to concern for others that we can really understand the meaning of life. Selfish concern for ourselves is a dying. Caring is living.

This is the radical message of Christ. "I tell you solemnly, in so far as you did this to one of the least of these brothers of mine, you did it unto me," Our Lord said.

We live fully only as we care about others. This radical Christianity we are called to follow demands of us caring about others; more than that, loving others. We serve Christ only in so far as we serve others.

We are called to love all people, for this is what caring means. And radically we are called to love not only those who love us and do good to us but our enemies, those who do evil to us, as well.

And as we serve Christ only in so far as we serve the least of those among us, so we finally love God only as much as the one we love least.

All right, no one said the following of Christ would be easy. No one ever doubted we are weak and we fail, that all of us, every one of us, are sinners; no one ever doubted that, least of all God, who has known us from all eternity, who cannot be surprised or disappointed that we sometimes fail.

But we can care, we can reach out our lives towards others, we can learn to weep when another is hurt, feel the humiliation when another suffers indignities, we can learn to care. We must learn to care. For only in caring do we really live.

CHAPTER 2

Looking Out for Number One

"I believe in looking out for No. 1. No one else is going to do it for you. You may not like it but that's my philosophy and I learned it by experience.

"I saw what happened to my father because he didn't do it and I made up my mind the same thing wasn't going to happen to me.

"So you can lecture me but you won't change me. I'm going to look out for No. 1."

You won't get any argument out of me if you say you believe in looking out for No. 1. I not only won't argue against it, I'm for it.

The difference I might have with some people, though, would be in determining who No. 1 is.

Gayle Sayers, the great All-American back who set pro football records with the Chicago Bears, put it right when he gave the order in his life—First, God, then other people, then me, he said.

The trouble some people have results from moving themselves into the number one position. If, when you say you believe in looking out for No. 1, you mean yourself, and that's probably what most people mean when they say it, then you're mixed up in your priorities.

When I say you must place God and other people before yourself, I'm not just speaking piously. That's what you must do if you've ordered your life properly. God and his laws must come first. Then we must be concerned about others. Finally we must be concerned about ourselves.

While the order is right, all three come together. Scripture tells us we must love God and we must love our neighbor as ourselves. They are all three united, a part of one whole. You get it wrong if you come to despise yourself, think that you are nothing. You're something and you have to keep that in mind. We are told we should love others as we love ourselves; if we don't love ourselves then how are we going to love others? We must love God, first of all, but our love of others and our love for ourselves comes with our love of God.

If through Scripture we learn we must love God and love others, we can observe it is a principle to be found true in common experience.

Because there is objective truth, although modern society sometimes tries to deny it, there are principles all people are called to accept.

Those who ignore God, place themselves ahead of God's law, court disaster. The natural law deals with mankind as mankind really is. The laws of God are always, in effect, declarations of the importance of individual human dignity. The Ten Commandments are finally admonitions of respect for individual rights and dignity in a context of belief in God.

If we place ourselves ahead of other people we are not only acting in conflict with God's admonition that we must love others as we love ourselves, but on a human level we are setting ourselves up for a fall.

I once knew a young man whose greatest interest

was in his own advancement. He undercut those who were his immediate superiors, going to those over them, currying favor with those at the top. He advanced, too, moved rapidly in the organization. But when he finally got into a position of real authority he discovered that his success in his new position depended on the support of those over whom he'd run roughshod in his climb to the top. He failed miserably, finally lost his position, because in placing himself first he had ignored the rights and dignities of others.

So on a human level, it is a bad idea to place yourself ahead of all else. We live not alone but among others and we are finally dependent on one another. When we ignore the dignity and rights of others, we create a disorder in the community that finally harms ourselves.

I'm not arguing that you should place God and other people before yourself because it is in your own self-interest to do so. If you placed God and others before yourself just because it works to your advantage to do so then that would be placing yourself first.

But what I am saying is that because this is the proper ordering, because it is true that we must place God and others before ourselves, when we disregard that truth we are harmed.

CHAPTER 3

Watch Where You Throw Your Chewing Gum

People want to be caring people.

I've learned this from thousands of people I've known. There's a popular view that most people are selfish, interested only in themselves.

But that's just not true. Most people are really concerned about other people. If you want evidence for this then just look at your own community. You'll find a hundred ways that people are showing they care about other people. You'll find it in the United Way, in the many charities that exist to help people in need.

Parents want to teach their children to be caring persons and I receive letters from them, asking how they can help their children to become unselfish.

Sometimes people act in ways that may not seem to be caring. But I think it is more often because they have not learned how, rather than they do not want to be caring people.

Someone asked me how you can teach children to be caring persons. I said you should teach them not to throw their chewing gum where someone might step on it.

That may sound like a flippant answer but it really isn't. I didn't mean it to be funny, I meant it seriously. It is about as basic an example of how to be caring as you could find.

Caring about people doesn't just mean you should do something *for* them, you need to be certain you don't do anything *to* them. Our acts are not isolated from others but almost everything we do affects others.

We learn early in our lives to think about whether what we are doing might harm us. Even the smallest children come to understand, often by experience, that you must not touch things that are hot because that can hurt you.

As we grow older we come automatically to think of the consequences of our actions to ourselves. But the caring person does not limit the consideration of the consequences of his actions to his own self but thinks of the consequences to others.

That's the way it should be. We must always in all we do think of other people. If we marry, then we do in our love expand our consciousness to include our wife or husband; when we have children we expand that consciousness to include them. It is also expanded to include friends, relatives, neighbors.

But if we are really to become caring persons we must include everyone.

There's a good example of how this must be done in the world today. We live in an affluence that is beyond even the imagination of millions of people in the world. Because we are able to afford luxuries, because we can afford to buy great supplies of food, because we can pay for the higher costs of energy, we are likely to think we have a right to do so.

But we cannot isolate ourselves from others in the world. If we waste food when there are people starving in the world then we have sinned against other people. When we recklessly use the sources of energy, because we can afford to pay for them, we are using resources in the world that cannot be replenished. Our indulgence for our own comfort and own pleasure is not just something that concerns ourselves, it concerns all of the people in the world.

This isn't something that people find easy to understand. People who have compassion for other people, who are generous towards those in need, who want to help the starving people in the world and give to those agencies that bring help to the suffering, think of this as fulfilling their responsibility to others.

And yet many, even among the good and the compassionate, may not think of their own actions as involving other people. They must, if they are to be caring, adjust their thinking to consider the consequences of all they do. They must come to understand that if they choose the luxury automobile that uses more gasoline than other cars, they are not making a decision that concerns only themselves but a decision that deprives someone else. When we sit down to a table of more food than we can possibly eat, we are depriving others of what may be a necessity.

I'm not saying we must deprive ourselves because others are deprived. A life of poverty chosen for spiritual reasons has purpose. I'm not certain when I read that someone in a prominent position has adopted a life of poverty or placed himself on a diet only equal to that of the poorest that this is necessarily good. Especially I'm wary of this when it is accompanied with a great deal of publicity. It is not impossible that those who do this may have exchanged an excessive appetite for the comforts of life for public acclaim. That may be an unjustified judgment, though, so I really shouldn't think it.

But anyhow, that's not what I'm talking about. I'm not suggesting that because people are starving in Bangladesh that you should choose starvation for yourself.

But what I am talking about is a concern you must have that your actions do not contribute to conditions that harm others. You can live well without living luxuriously. You can eat well without depriving yourself of a proper diet and without wasting food. You can take advantage of your means of transportation without doing so wastefully.

All that the caring person is asked to do is to consider others, to understand that we cannot act in isolation from other people.

Be careful that you do not throw your chewing gum where someone might step on it. Learn that and carry it on to all that you do and you cannot help being a caring person.

CHAPTER 4

My Friend Mr. Swadee

The loneliness of older people results in great part from the fact that they have lost their friends through death and there's now no one with whom they can talk.

A man from Louisville wrote to me of the loneliness he experienced and the sense of uselessness he had. And then a few months later he wrote a happy letter:

"There is a program here in which we become honorary grandparents for young people. Once a week I go to a school where I talk with the students and help teach them something about carpentry. I feel useful again."

Loneliness is the product of not caring. When there are people who care then they can dispel the loneliness of others. If we care about people then we will not allow them to be lonely.

Old Mr. Swadee was a round little man, his hair white. Mornings he left home, carrying a big basket of coffee cakes Mrs. Swadee had baked before sunrise. It was, so far as I know, the only way they had to support themselves.

But afternoons Mr. Swadee was free. The other men of the neighborhood were all at work. So Mr. Swadee talked to me. He had a heavy German accent; he talked of the Old Country and he told some remarkable tales.

There was the time when he was on the way from the Old Country. The ship had run into a terrible storm. It

tossed and turned and there was a danger of it cap-
sizing. The helmsman could not hold the ship on
course and the captain said, in desperation, "How I
wish we had Billy Swadee to get us through the
storm." And someone said, "Did you say Billy Swadee,
Captain? He happens to be on this very ship, headed
for a new life in America."

So the captain sent for Billy. "Billy," he said.
"Thank God you were on my ship when I needed you.
You're the only man who can pull us through this
storm."

So Billy took off his coat, took the helm. "Don't
worry, Captain. I've seen worse storms than this."
And when the ship was safely through, the Captain
shook his hand and said, "Billy, you have saved us
all." And Billy said, "That's all right, Captain. I was
glad to help."

Billy's stories were told with a heavy German accent,
so heavy that some grownups said you could hardly
understand anything he said. But I didn't want to try
the accent in telling his story, not only because it
would have been difficult to catch, but most of all
because I didn't hear it as accented. I heard it just as a
story told to me by an old gentleman who was my
friend.

It was just one of a hundred stories like it, all of
which had Billy Swadee as the hero. Long before there
was Walter Mitty there was Billy Swadee, living even
more daringly, more heroically, than Walter Mitty
ever would have dared.

Lots of the kids made fun of Billy Swadee. They'd laugh at me, say I was a sucker for Billy Swadee's tall stories. I never called him Billy, he was Mr. Swadee to me, and I believed all the stories he told me even if I realized they probably weren't true.

Once I told my mother how other kids said I was a sucker for Mr. Swadee's tall stories. My dad and my mother were friends of the Swadees, every-morning coffee cake customers. My mother told me that Mr. Swadee was a storyteller, as Aesop and Frank Baum who wrote the Oz stories, were storytellers.

But, I asked, "Are they tall stories?" She thought awhile and said, "Mr. Swadee is not telling you lies, he is telling you stories and they are wonderful stories."

So it didn't matter what anyone else said, I became an even more willing listener to Mr. Swadee. Sometimes, although I knew he wasn't telling me lies, the stories got pretty big. Like the time he was traveling through Texas and the stage coach on which he was traveling was attacked by a hoop snake.

The driver saw the snake along the side of the road and he took the whip to speed up the horses. But that snake just took his tail in his mouth and rolled down the hill, coming at such a speed he was gaining on them.

"Someone help," the stage driver called down. "That hoop snake is going to catch up with us, kill the horses and kill us all."

"Slow down a little," Billy called up. "Let that snake come alongside and I'll take care of him."

He opened the door of the stage coach and waited. He pulled out his hunting knife and when the hoop snake rolled by he leaned out the door and he slashed at the snake. He cut it right in half but the snake let go of his tail and in his dying moment struck at Billy, catching him midway on his knee-high boot.

"The driver pulled up and I jerked that boot off my foot," Billy told me. "And then right before my eyes that boot swelled up twice the size."

"Really, Mr. Swadee?" asked.

He laughed, "Really," he said.

Mr. Swadee died one winter. My parents said he never dressed warmly enough for the winter.

They brought his body to the little home. I went in to see him and although I'd known he was a little man he seemed smaller than I'd ever remembered him being. If it had not been for the gray hair and the little white mustache he would have looked like a child.

Mrs. Swadee stood beside me. "You were his best friend," she said. I'd never thought that I could be a friend to a grownup and it seemed strange to me that she should call me his friend. The friends of grownups are other grownups and I was a little boy but I knew how I would miss him and I liked the thought we were not just a grownup and a little boy who listened to him but that we were friends.

But Mr. Swadee wasn't the only grownup I listened to when I was a boy. I liked to listen to old people talk; they knew things I could never know unless I listened to them. There was Uncle Jake Francis who had taken a bullet in his head at the battle of Bull Run, a bullet they had not been able to remove, that was still there. He let me feel the place on his head where it had entered and he said he was one of the few veterans of the war who carried a souvenir with him wherever he went. Old Mr. Boehringer was another Civil War veteran I knew. He'd come for a couple of weeks to visit relatives a few blocks up Walnut Street from our home.

He had a long white beard and he didn't say much at all. But he'd come out on the porch to sit in the afternoon and when I saw him there I'd go to the house and sit on the step. He never told me any stories, he hardly talked at all except to say it was hot or it looked like rain but I'd sit there, looking at him, thinking that maybe he'd seen Mr. Lincoln or General Grant, although he never said he had.

Late afternoons I'd go to Doc Saul's bowling alley. The reason I offered was I wanted to watch the ball scores come in on the ticker. I lived and died with the Cincinnati Reds, mostly died because after just missing beating out the Cardinals when I was nine, the Reds slipped further and further down in the standings.

But if waiting for the ball scores was the first reason I went to Doc Saul's bowling alley, there was another reason. I could listen to what grownups said. I was the only boy around and no one ever said anything to me but the men talked to each other and I listened. Not everything I heard were things my parents would want me to hear but it was grownup talk and just hearing it helped me know things I had not known before.

It was my interest in baseball that made me decide I

wanted to be a newspaperman. I thought that if I learned to be a newspaperman maybe some day when Jack Ryder was too old to cover the Reds for the Cincinnati *Enquirer* I could get a chance to write about baseball.

I was 15 when I went down to the paper, walked up to the editorial room, asked for the editor. Ray Steinmetz came out and I had practiced what I would say. "I want to be a newspaperman," I said. "I want to learn. I'll sweep the floors, empty the wastebaskets, I'll do anyting you want me to do if you'll just let me stay around and learn to be a newspaperman."

Ray told me later that the last thing he'd wanted was to have a kid around but he said, "We have someone to do the janitor work. But if you want to learn to be a newspaperman we'll give you a chance."

Then he said, "Supposing you just go out and get us an interesting story. You decide what it will be."

And I remembered an old friend, Mr. Venable. He had been a slave when the Civil War began and when the Union troops came through and told all the slaves they were free, he had stayed with the troops, cooking for them, helping them out.

So I hurried to his home and I took down all the things that he told me: how it was to be a slave, how it was to be free. So the very first thing I ever wrote as a newspaperman was a story told by one of the old men I used to listen to and the newspaper carried it on the front page. I remember almost every word of it; I remember even the typographical error. I'd written he had brushed away "an annoying fly" as he talked and it came out "an annopling fly."

Listening to older people talk was something I did for myself but a few years later I understood a dimension of it I had not understood before. I was still in my teens when my Uncle Hugh died and because it seemed not right that Aunt Clara should return alone to Atlanta with Uncle Hugh's body, I went along on the last train.

Old Mr. Hadaway was there, sad that he should have outlived his son. We were there for less than a week but while we were there, he talked to me almost all the time. He talked of his childhood, of what it was like when he was a young man; he told me a thousand things and one day while I was listening to him, I understood something I had not really understood before.

He was an old man. He didn't have long to live. There were things he wanted to remember, things he wanted to say, before it was too late to say them. His days were running out and there was so much he had to say.

I had thought my listening was for myself but then I understood my listening helped the one who was talking to me. His family, his neighbors had heard every story he had ever told but I was someone who wanted to hear him talk.

And then I understood how I was a friend to Mr. Swadee.

CHAPTER 5

A Valentine for Mary Etta

Sometimes when people think about caring they think about caring for those in far off places.

That's one important way of caring. We should care about the starving in the drought areas of Sub-Sahara Africa, about the victims of an earthquake in Nicaragua.

But caring must begin with the people you meet every day.

Caring about people is something you learn. Selfishness is closer to our flawed nature than caring about other people.

My mother taught me a lesson about caring when I was in the fourth grade—taught us all, for she involved my brother and sister in her plan, too.

Each year we had a Valentine box and during the week we dropped in Valentines for our classmates. Then on Valentine's Day the box was opened up and the Valentines given out.

We were always required to make out Valentines for each of our classmates so that we'd leave no one out. But as we were preparing our Valentine cards, I set aside the prettiest one for a little girl named Betty whom I especially admired.

I must have said something about how many cards this pretty little girl would get for mother asked, "Is there anyone in your class who won't get many Valentines?"

I didn't have to think about that. There was no doubt about who would get the fewest Valentines. It would be Mary Etta. Mary Etta was really a pretty child with dark hair and pink cheeks but she wasn't like other children. She lived with her grandmother in a little house that wasn't much more than a shack. I don't know what had happened to her parents. She didn't talk to us and we didn't talk to her. She was dressed in flowered print dresses that had obviously been made by her grandmother. In a day in which little girls wore their hair short and fluffy, her hair was long and braided.

I told my Mother I knew who would get the fewest, probably get only my Valentine because we were the only children who had to give everyone Valentines.

"All right, then," she said, "we'll see that she gets some."

We all signed Valentines, my own with my name, but the others my brother, my sister, mother and I signed with names like classmate, a friend, fellow student, making the handwriting a little different each time. When we finished we had a whole stack of Valentines for Mary Etta.

The day for opening the Valentine box came. I looked over at Mary Etta as Miss Hurd announced she was going to open the box and give out the Valentines. She was looking very hard into her reading book, acting as if she wasn't interested. Miss Hurd called off the names and the one receiving the Valentine came forward to get it.

One of the first was for Mary Etta and she went

forward, her face solemn. Before all were distributed she had been called to the front of the room as often as the most popular of the children and when the very last Valentine was for her she walked up front, trying to hold back a smile that wouldn't be held back, her ruddy cheeks pinker than ever.

I don't know what happened to Mary Etta. That spring she left school, perhaps to go to live with her own parents. I don't know because none of us ever knew anything about Mary Etta. But I'll bet wherever she is she still remembers that day in the fourth grade at Kyle School when she was the little girl who got as many Valentines as the most popular little girls in the room.

I know I remember it, remember the happiness it gave me just seeing her happy; remember a lesson I was taught about caring for people, especially those people others care about least.

CHAPTER 6

Letting Children Be Persons

"My greatest sorrow is that my son, reared as a good Catholic, educated in Catholic schools, no longer practices his faith."

There are hundreds of letters like this in my mail. But the letters are not just about children who have abandoned their faith but children who have rejected moral values, chosen a way of life different than that of parents.

In a way, I suppose it is always true that young people often disappoint their parents. It has happened in all generations, I would think. But it probably is happening now more than ever.

There may be more Catholic young people who are not practicing their faith today than there were in other generations. But it happened before.

One of the soundest Catholics I know is a man who, in his college years, not only abandoned his Catholic faith but became a strong opponent of the Catholic Church.

I didn't have any contact with his parents in those days but they are the kind of Catholics who must have been greatly distressed by the choices their son was making.

But about a decade after his rebellion he was back in the Church and not just a nominal Catholic but an enthusiastic Catholic. He didn't stop at his rebellion but went on and somewhere along the way became a Catholic through conviction.

Another friend who wound up in his thirties as a daily communicant, a Catholic by conviction, was a man who for nearly twenty years never even got to Mass. When he came back it wasn't because of any trauma in his life—I hear people saying that those who leave the Church will come back when they run into some tragedy in life and realize their need for religion. That may be true, it just happens I don't know of any cases like that but I don't doubt it happens. This fellow came back because he started thinking about it, started reading about the Church, discovered the Church he rebelled against when he was a teenager wasn't the Church at all.

That doesn't mean all those people who have slipped away from the Catholic Church today will some day later on be coming back. There's no way I could know that. But what I tell people who come to me is that I think they shouldn't get up tight about it.

What I've observed, not just in relation to this problem but in relation to most problems that are similar, is that when people get up tight they are less likely to change the minds of those who are doing something they don't like than they are to confirm the ones they are trying to dissuade in the decisions they have made.

Pride is a very powerful human emotion. If, by angry words, you create a situation in which the one you are trying to convince is placed in such a position that to come to your way of thinking would demand a humbling of self, then you make it more difficult. I've seen people who realized they had made a mistake but who could simply not admit it because it became a matter of pride.

What has to be done for those who leave the practice of their faith is to leave them a way to come home.

I've had letters from people who said that when their children stopped practicing their faith they simply disowned them. One man wrote, "I just told him to get out. I told him when he came to his senses, got back to the practice of his faith, we'd be glad to have him back but until he did that, he was no longer our son."

First of all, I can't understand how any parent could do that. Our children are our children. If what our children have done is something we wish they had not done then, of course, we are sad. But how parents could possibly cut off children because they had done something the parents disapproved is beyond my comprehension.

Not only is this kind of reaction a violation of the requirements of love, it is simply stupid. It would seem almost impossible for the child to return to a home where the door had been so firmly closed.

It seems to me many of the difficulties between parents and children derive from a misunderstanding of who our children are. Our children are persons. They are not our possessions, they are not intended to become facsimilies of ourselves. They are from the very beginning human beings to be respected as persons.

Our instruction, our discipline must never be to force them to conform to us but to realize themselves more fully as persons. Because we do have experiences they do not have, because we have learned some things by living, there is guidance we can offer our children.

But some parents make the mistake of looking on their children as their possessions—"He is my son, by God, and he's going to do what I tell him to do"—and so what they set out to do is not to allow the child to become the person he or she is but try to make that child into a facsimile of the parent. That doesn't work precisely because the child is another person and, being another person, must realize the person he or she is.

Sometimes parents look on their children as their own second chance for living. The mother who always wanted to be the most popular girl and never made it wants her daughter to be the most popular girl she never was.

I know a woman who married just at the time she was preparing to be a classical singer. She had children, ended her dream of being a concert artist, maybe even an artist at the Metropolitan Opera, but always mourned what she considered had been the sacrifice she made for her family. When her daughter showed some signs of talent the mother determined her daughter would give her the second chance for what she had dreamed about.

Her daughter did have talent but her mother's dream was not her own. Because she was an obedient daughter she did what her mother wanted her to do, studied at Julliard, prepared for the career that would give her mother a second chance.

Years later I ran into her by chance in New York City. She had gone on from Julliard to study under one of the nation's finest teachers—and married him, had a family but no career and was very happy. It was only the death of her mother that had freed her from the obligation that had been imposed on her of living her mother's life and not her own.

Our children are not our possessions; they are our responsibility but the responsibility is one of helping them become more fully who they are.

If we expect our children will be just what we want them to be, then we are building ourselves a disappointment. And if somehow we force our children to become facsimilies of ourselves then we are building disappointment for our children.

Not that it doesn't sometimes happen, happen happily for both parents and children. We all know young people who move into the family businesses and sons and daughters who follow the professions of their parents and are happy doing it. That isn't strange— children admire their parents, may come to want to do what their parents have done. But it should come naturally, it should come through the son or daughter, not because the parents wish it.

The son of the best doctor in my home town decided he wanted to be a doctor, too. There's no doubt he became a doctor because he wanted to be a doctor and he wanted to be a doctor because he had seen what great good his father had done.

That made Doc Jones—that wasn't his real name— happy. Doc Jones was coming to a time he needed to take it a little easier. It gave him a great happiness to think it would soon be Dr. Jones and Son. Only that wasn't the way his son had wanted it. He didn't want to be young Doc Jones. He didn't want to take over his father's practice. If he returned to his home town he knew that he'd always be his father's son. He wanted to be himself. He admired his father, he was motivated by the example of his father, but he didn't want to be his father. He didn't want to be Young Doc Jones, the son of Old Doc Jones.

He went off to a state far away. His father was not just disappointed, he was hurt; he never really did understand; he saw the action of his son as a rejection of himself. And that wasn't it at all. it wasn't a rejection of his father but an assertion of himself that made it necessary for young Doc Jones to go far away.

Old Doc Jones is gone now. A young doctor he brought in when he realized his son wasn't going to come join him has the office he once had and old Doc Jones's sign has been replaced. Old Doc had dreamed that sign would still be there when he was gone but that was the way it couldn't be, not if his son was to realize his own self. Young Doc Jones is a very successful doctor, a skilled surgeon as his father was, and he has sons of his own. It is to be hoped that he remembers and that he won't want his son to continue his life —but the way people are, he may have forgotten.

When along the way do you start treating children as if they were persons? I think it must be from infancy. If you think you can wait until your children are teenagers to start letting them make the kinds of decisions that come from their own convictions, you are deceiving yourself.

Responsible parenthood requires teaching self-reliance. And that begins from infancy. That doesn't mean you don't offer guidance, that you don't insist on discipline, that you don't pass on values—all of these are necessary if a child is to move to self-reliance and to the fullness of personhood. But what is done should never be done because you insist your child be exactly the way you want him or her to be, but because you want to help your child to realize the fullness of his or her personality. You do that by respecting your child's dignity as a person.

When children don't turn out as parents wish them, you often hear parents lamenting, "What did we do wrong? Where did we fail?" That wail comes often when children enter their twenties and parents realize those children have discarded values the parents hold dear.

But the questions are wrong. What young people do is their own responsibility. It is natural for parents to lament but the responsibility is not their own. Even if they did make mistakes, even if they should have handled things differently, it does no good to wail. We're not the only influences in our children's lives. There's a time in the life of young people that peer example is more influential than parental example. When our children reach maturity they are responsible for their own lives.

But our response must always be one of love. There's nothing wrong in allowing our children to know of our disappointment; chances are they'd realize it anyhow, but we must not dwell on our disappointment. Rather, most of all, we must show our love.

When disappointed parents come to me I just tell them to love their children, always offer them acceptance even if they cannot accept the lifestyle their children have chosen. Love your children and never stop loving them.

And be willing to learn from them, too. There are decisions our children make that we can and should regret. But we must be careful that we do not confuse what is of substance with what is not.

There are things that we have wanted that it may very well be we should not have wanted. Along with what is really important we have probably gathered into one package what was not important. Our children may have recognized as false, values that we thought were important—worldly success and comfort being obvious examples that a great many of us have packaged along with values of real importance.

One of the most difficult transitions we have in life is the one of realizing our children are grown up, are adults as we are. It is natural that we see them as our children; they are at once the infants we held in our arms, the toddlers we helped take their first steps, the chldren we watched go off to school, the little boys and girls growing into adolescence, the young people they were—it is a difficult leap to seeing them as adults. Every day we meet young people, in their twenties, in their thirties, and we see them as adults and mature, but our children we still see as children.

But we must see them as young adults, as persons, and we must pray for them, love them and open ourselves to learn from them, too.

CHAPTER 7

The Day I Didn't Turn Up the Alley

It was a different kind of a letter.

"My problem may not seem like much of a problem compared to that of other people. Our children are good children but they are ashamed of their father's work.

"He drives a garbage truck. It is a good job, he has more responsibility than just driving a garbage truck. My daughter and my son have friends whose fathers are professional people or have businesses.

"I tell them their father's work is honest work, that it must be done. They understand that but still they are ashamed of him. I understand how they feel but yet it hurts me and although my husband does not show it, I'm sure it hurts him, too."

Most of the important things you learn in life you are unaware you are learning. But sometimes there are lessons that you realize you are learning and know exactly what it is you are learning. That happened to me one day on Mulberry Street when I didn't go into the alley.

Grandma Smallenbarger wasn't really our grandmother. She lived across the street from us and she was our friend; not only the friend of our parents but of all the kids in the family. She was especially my friend because she'd listen each Saturday afternoon when my brother and I came home from the matinee at the Colonial to my recitation of what had happened in the latest Tom Tyler, Bob Steele, Buck Jones, Hoot Gibson, Ken Maynard or Tim McCoy western.

She couldn't really have been interested but she'd let me tell the whole story, get excited at the critical moments, laugh at the funny parts. She was my friend.

Mr. Smallenberger was not well, had not been well for a long time, and Grandma Smallenberger took in washing to help support the two of them. When I was about nine she asked me if I'd deliver the laundry to her two customers.

I would have been glad to do it just because it was Grandma Smallenberger who asked but there was a reward, too. For picking up the dirty laundry and delivering the washed and ironed to the Peters' home, I got 10 cents. For doing the same for the Mott sisters, I got 15 cents. I don't know why the difference, the Peters' home was twice as far away, but I was paid by the customers and that was what they paid.

I put the laundry in my red wagon and the delivery was easy. The chance to earn a quarter a week in those days was something any kid would be glad to have. Week after week, I'd deliver the laundries, pick them up. As the weeks became years, I found other ways to make money, a paper route, caddying, finally working at the newspaper, actually writing a summer sports column for the daily newspaper. But I kept on delivering the laundry for Grandma Smallenbarger.

I was still delivering the laundry when I was a junior in high school. The red wagon had grown old and the wheels squeaked beyond any possible cure by 3-in-1 Oil. I tried carrying the laundry baskets but they were too big, not too heavy, just too cumbersome to be carried.

The laundry I delivered to the Mott sisters was only about eight blocks—three blocks up Walnut and five over to Grant. But the Peters' laundry took me down Mulberry street, right to Main street, close to the center of town.

I was sixteen years old. Because I was already writing for the newspaper I had a feeling I was more mature than most; I enjoyed the attention it gave me and when Bob Newhall, the sportscaster at WLW in Cincinnati did a piece about the young sportswriter in Troy, I thought I'd achieved a kind of fame. I found myself embarrassed to be pulling a little red wagon with a laundry basket on it right into the center of town.

I was pulling the red wagon with the Peters' laundry on it up Mulberry one Saturday morning. I kept hoping I'd not meet anyone. But about a block from Main street I looked ahead and I saw two girls and a boy just turning onto Mulberry. One of the girls was a pretty blonde-haired girl who had just moved to town I thought I'd like to meet; the other two kids I already knew.

They hadn't seen me. They were standing talking to each other. There was an alley right beside me. I had a feeling close to panic. I thought if I turned into the alley, went down it, they wouldn't see me. I almost did it but I didn't.

I made a quick and conscious decision. I thought there was nothing to be ashamed about in pulling a red wagon with laundry on it. If anyone thought less of me because of that then it was their problem, not mine. So I didn't turn off in the alley. I pulled my red wagon on up the street. When they passed me I spoke to them. I heard one of them giggle but I was surprised to discover it didn't embarrass me.

When I delivered the laundry, I pulled the red wagon back home. As I went home I thought about the experience. I was sorry I'd even thought about turning up that alley.

Then I said to myself, "You learned an important lesson today. Some day you'll look back on it and think you learned one of the most important lessons of your life today."

And I believe that now.

CHAPTER 8
The Man They Called Pop

The hints of explanation we get in life often come to us most clearly in the lives other people live.

We are all of us witnesses to what we believe, what we hold to be most important.

And in life we sometimes encounter star witnesses for goodness, for caring.

When he died the whole town mourned. Everyone called him "Pop" but not me, I called him Mr. Dixon.

He came to town as the pastor of the First Baptist Church. He was different. The previous pastor has been a tall, dignified man with a solemn but kindly face, who wore dark suits and combed a full head of hair back in a pompadour. Mr. Dixon dressed informally, had a shining bald head that was always exposed to the elements because he never wore a hat and he didn't smile but grinned.

There wasn't another clergyman in town in any way like him. Monsignor Mentink, who had been at St. Patrick's for 30 years, was loved but he was a solemn man, too. As a matter of fact, preachers and priests were expected to be both solemn and dignified. Mr. Dixon was neither.

This was in the 1930s and you have to understand the importance of Mr. Dixon not wearing a hat. Today men don't wear hats much at all. In those days all men wore hats; boys wore caps or tobaggons. In all the towns there was no one who went bareheaded except

Mr. Dixon. This was affront enough but the fact that he was so bald made it even more scandalous.

It may be difficult to understand now but Mr. Dixon not wearing a hat became a matter of great importance. Chances are no one said anything to Mr. Dixon about it. If they had he would have just laughed. But the people talked about it among themselves and there were some who were members of the First Baptist Church who said he ought to be told that a preacher was expected to wear a hat.

But the scandal of Mr. Dixon's bareheadedness was almost forgotten as he settled down into the town. He became less comprehensible the more people learned about him.

For one thing, early risers reported seeing him walking around the streets of the town at 5 A.M. They would look out the window and there he would be, striding down the street, his bald head exposed, no matter what the weather.

Someone asked him about it, making it casual, and he grinned and said, "Oh, sure, I like to get up early and walk a couple of miles before breakfast." That was almost too much, preachers were expected to stay at home or be at the church office. If they were seen in public then it was at special affairs of civic interest. No one in town got up early in the morning to walk a couple of miles before breakfast and if anyone had, he would have been thought peculiar. But for a preacher to do it wasn't just peculiar, it was downright unbelievable.

He had arrived in early fall and winter came early that year. Then it was people realized the new Baptist preacher not only didn't wear a hat, he didn't even wear an overcoat. It could be snowing and there he was, walking right downtown, no overcoat, the snowflakes melting on top of his bald head, grinning and calling out greetings to everyone he met—not just Baptists but everyone.

He was a scandal but the town hadn't seen anything yet. The First Baptist Church had a meeting room. The Ladies Aid met there and the BYPU on Sunday evenings. There was a piano to accompany the singing of hymns but there were no social meetings there. It was for the discussion of serious matters and for devotionals.

Mr. Dixon changed that. He did it himself without consulting the deacons of the church. He announced it was going to be a place for the young people to meet. He made clear he wasn't just talking about the young people of the First Baptist Church but for anyone who wanted to come.

There weren't many young people who came the first Saturday night. But those who came had a good time. There were no devotions, nothing even suggesting church. There were games, there was singing of "Down By the Old Mill Stream" and "Sweet Adeline." Those who were there were at first a little uncomfortable, not certain it was quite right to be having fun in church, but soon everyone was laughing and having a good time.

More young people came the next week, young people from all the churches, even some Catholics. Some people were suspicious, they thought the new Baptist preacher was trying to proselytize and in a town in which Baptists were Baptists, Methodists were Methodists, Episcopalians were Episcopalians and Catholics were Catholics, that didn't sit well at all.

But the Baptists were concerned because that accusation obviously wasn't true. He not only wasn't trying to make other young people into Baptists, he didn't even mention religion at all.

There were other shocks to come. When a girl in town, not really in the town but across the B&O tracks in Culbertson Heights, got in what was euphemistically called "trouble," he helped her. She wasn't even one of the people in his church but he butted in and made arrangements for her and when she came back in a few months he took her into his home for a while.

It soon became evident that Mr. Dixon was going to butt in whenever any young people were in difficulty. A lot of people said he ought to be spending his time with decent young people instead of getting mixed up with the bad kids.

Even his sermons were scandalous. He didn't reserve his sermons to proper biblical subjects. He talked about things that were happening in the town and in the country.

There were a lot of people who said he wasn't a preacher at all, just a meddler. He must have heard that because he told the people a story one Sunday—

that was another thing wrong with him, he kept telling funny stories in church, stories that made you want to laugh even if you knew you weren't supposed to laugh in church.

"There was a preacher once," he said, "who was down on sin and people liked that. He denounced murder and an old lady down front called out, 'Amen, Preacher, you're really preaching!' He denounced adultery and the lady called out, 'Amen, Preacher, you're really preaching!' He denounced drunkenness and the lady called out again, 'Amen, Preacher, you're really preaching!' And then he denounced the use of snuff and the old lady stood up, shook her fist, and shouted, 'You've done stopped preaching and started meddling.'"

And there was no doubt Mr. Dixon was a meddler. There was nothing that happened in town that he didn't care about. The first talk I ever gave in my life I gave at his church, at his urging because he heard me express my ideas and he said I should express them in public. It was a talk against racial prejudice. That Mr. Dixon, he even cared about Negroes.

The years went by and the town got used to Mr. Dixon. But more than used to him. They got to love him. Not everybody, of course, some people still thought he didn't act the way a preacher should.

He expanded his youth club and moved it into a building downtown on the square where young people could come to dance, to play pool and ping pong. By that time his critics had given up, nothing surprised them, not even a preacher who encouraged dancing and pool and even cards.

The youth center was called "The Rec" and it was the place young people went in a town where before there hadn't been anything for young people to do. The center had become such a big project that it required his full time and so Mr. Dixon resigned his pastorate and became the full-time director of "The Rec."

I was away from the town at that time, the way other young men were away at war, so I don't know when it was that the kids stopped calling him Mr. Dixon and started calling him "Pop." It wouldn't have been something he would have minded, he probably was glad for it; after all, he had insisted that we not call him Reverend, the way we had called other preachers before him, but just call him Mr. Dixon.

It was more than twenty years later that I got back to my home town and by that time everyone called him "Pop," not just the kids but the grownups, too. Chances are many of the grownups had been his kids years before.

When I think of caring I always think of Mr. Dixon. He wasn't just a preacher who taught religion, he was a man who lived it. He lived it because he really did care about other people and, because he cared, he had to help anyone who needed help.

When he died the whole town mourned. A lot of people had forgotten he ever had been a preacher, he was a preacher in town only six or seven years, he was

"Pop" for nearly thirty. But he was a minister for Christ all the days of his life, that grinning man with the shining bald head and the cheery greeting for everyone, that meddler into people's troubles: he made Christ live for people in a way no one else in town ever had before.

CHAPTER 9
A Miracle Named Rose

The people who write to me have real problems. I think we do not really realize how many people there are who are suffering among us.

But what astounds me so often is how people who carry the heaviest burdens are sometimes the most likely to be concerned about other people.

I have known some remarkable people but none more remarkable than Rose Mort.

A smiling, redhaired woman, she could only be described as vivacious. She was constantly busy doing things for other people. I can think of no one I've ever known who was more directed towards others than Rose.

We met when I did a radio program called "Interesting Neighbors," in which I introduced people in the community who were doing things of importance. We became close friends after that and for the rest of the years of her life she involved me in the many things she was doing. I'd get a letter, telling me I'd been named to this or that committee or board, and that on this date or that I was expected to be somewhere. When I moved more than 600 miles away she still counted on me and I'd find myself driving from North Carolina to Lima, Ohio, because Rose asked me.

I read a lot but I found Rose always kept up with every important new book and she would be telling me what I should be reading or discussing with me the book I had just read.

She carried on correspondence with literally hundreds of persons across the country and her letters were, like Rose, laughing, happy letters. She collected jokes and her letters were filled with them.

She organized an annual picnic for handicapped persons and every Spring people would come from far off places to Lima for Rose's picnic. There would be among them the crippled, the blind, the deaf, the invalided and terminally ill. They came not to commiserate with each other—Rose wouldn't have allowed that—but to celebrate. Where Rose was there was laughter and song.

I never did understand how it was Rose collected her jokes. She couldn't have heard them because Rose Mort was totally deaf.

I knew how she kept up with the latest books for I sometimes delivered the huge Braille editions to her. Rose was totally blind but her fingers sped across the Braille; when she was caught up in real interest, her fingers moved so rapidly it seemed they barely touched the page.

She carried on her correspondence on an old typewriter. She had taught herself the keyboard and while sometimes in the exuberance of her writing she'd run off the page, there were remarkably few errors.

Her blind friends wrote to her in Braille but most of her correspondence was with sighted friends. She recruited friends to translate the letters into Braille—I was one of those who learned Braille to help her—or to simply "tell" her what the letters said.

Those who came to her picnics included many who were crippled and they related to Rose in a special way because Rose was crippled, too. The illness that had brought her blindness and deafness had forced a radical operation that had removed a leg. She had a wooden artificial leg and Rose, when she spoke of some good fortune, would laugh and say, "Knock on wood," and reach down to tap her leg.

She always had a special compassion for the ill, offering words of comfort, hope and courage, and in the last few years of her life she had a special understanding of the terminally ill for she battled for five years the cancer that eventually took her life.

If ever I've known a person who had a right to feel sorry for herself, Rose was the one. But I never heard a word of self-pity from her. She totally gave herself to others, she directed her thoughts away from herself.

If I'm vague about the illness that caused her problems—it would be wrong to call them handicaps because Rose didn't allow them to be that—it is because she never talked about it and I didn't ask her any questions.

She told me that the illness had come at a time I judged to be in her late teens because she spoke of how grateful she was that once in her life she had been able to see and to hear, that she could remember flowers and music. She counted that a blessing and she marveled that Helen Keller, who was one of the friends with whom she corresponded, could have accomplished so much never having been blessed at all with hearing or sight.

She spoke in a kind of a monotone, a little loudly. We carried on conversations. I would take her hand into my left hand, then with the index finger of my right hand write the letters into the palm of her hand. When she understood the word I was spelling she would close her hand on mine and I'd go to the next word. Usually the conversation went rapidly because I'd get only two or three letters written before she'd know what I was saying.

We became close friends and there were times she spoke seriously with me, especially in those last months before she died. She told me how grateful she was for all of the blessings she had received in her life.

I asked her once if she ever became depressed, felt sad about all she had been given to bear. Her face in thought was different than the smiling face that greeted everyone. She spoke to me very seriously.

"I really never allow myself sadness," she said. "Of course, I wish it could be different. But it isn't. I am the way I am. If I am going to do any good, it is as I am. If I am to be happy, it is as I am."

She had a favorite song. It was that song from "Carousel" that begins, "When I walk through the storm." Someone had given her the words and she repeated them often, they became almost a prayer for her.

She was a woman of great spirituality, although she

had no formal religious affiliation. During the time we were friends I had become a Catholic and she was greatly interested in this. One of the last times I saw her we talked about it. I'd written to her about why I had become a Catholic and she had started reading some Catholic books in Braille.

She said to me, "I would like to do what you did. I believe but my friends have all the funeral arrangements made and it would give them such problems."

She reached out for my hand, "Do you suppose in my heart is enough?"

I said, "I'm certain it is."

Rose Mort accomplished a lot with her life. She could have simply become an invalid, she could have closed in on herself and sat around waiting for death. There was reason enough for that and no one would have blamed her.

But she began where she was. "I'm a mess," she said laughing once. "But I'm my mess." She was grateful that once she had been able to see, to hear, to run. But while she made this her blessing it could have been an added cross. To be blind and to know what you could no longer see, to be deaf and remember the sound of music, could be a cause for greater sadness. She made it an occasion of joy.

What she accomplished would have been remarkable if she had not had her problems. When you consider how she did so much with so many difficulties it becomes almost miraculous.

And it was in a sense miraculous but only because

she made it so. The miracle of the life of Rose Mort was that she turned everything outward toward the world she could not see or hear so that she was a part of it, toward other people because she cared about them and wanted to share her blessings with them.

CHAPTER 10
When Friends Quarrel

"You tell us we should make up with people with whom we have quarrels. That's all very well but the one who should do the making up is the one who caused the quarrel in the first place."

She went on to tell me that she and her sister have not spoken in seven years. She told me how it happened and from what she told me I think it really was true her sister had caused the estrangement.

But that's irrelevant. It is the estrangement that is wrong, that must be ended, and that is the only relevancy.

The letters I receive tell me of many burdens people carry in their lives but there's one problem that I hear with such frequency that I'm certain that it must be found in the lives of millions of people.

It is the problem of separation from old friends, brothers or sisters, parents, children. Those who write to me are people who are sorry for the estrangement.

They tell me how it came about. I don't remember a letter in which the person writing to me thought that she or he had been responsible for the separation.

That may be the truth, too. It could well be that those who were not responsible for the estrangement are the ones who feel the burden of it most. It may be, too, that it is human nature to offer a kind of natural self-defense against any sense of responsibility for a separation we do not want. But I don't know that and it would not be fair of me to make that judgment.

In any case, it is irrelevant. The letters that come to me almost always say that friendship could be restored if only the other person showed some signs of contrition, if only the other person said he or she was sorry.

But that's not the way estrangement will end. What I tell those who want to restore friendship is that they must take the first step. It doesn't really matter who was to blame for the separation. It is the separation that is wrong.

If you are estranged from someone who should be close to you then you must go to that person or write to that person. You must say you want to be friends again, that for whatever you may have done you are sorry, that you want only for the separation to end.

Sometimes I get arguments. "But she really was to blame. Why shouldn't she be the one to say she is sorry? I'll forgive her but she should be the one who comes to me, not me to go to her."

That will only continue the separation. It's not what another did that is wrong in your life, it is the separation that is wrong. Maybe you are right, maybe another is the one who caused the separation. But that's in the past, the separation is in the present, and you are a cooperator in the separation by not doing all you can to end it. Take the first step, be the one who says you are sorry—for you are sorry about the separation.

And some say, "But what if I come to him, say I'm

sorry and I want to be friends, and he rejects me? That would only make it more difficult, to be rebuffed again.''

But it really wouldn't. It could be that the person from whom you are estranged may rebuff you, refuse to be friends again. That could happen, no reason to pretend it couldn't. But when you will have at least tried to end the separation, you will have at least offered your love and friendship, you will have broken the estrangement from your own side; instead of that making the separation more difficult, it is more likely to make it easier, for you'll no longer have a feeling of guilt about your own failure to end the separation. And you have opened the door. Perhaps the one from whom you are estranged just isn't psychologically prepared to respond at this moment, but you have made the way easier for him later and then the opportunity may arise for you to try again.

It is our own pride that perpetuates estrangements. That's as true of those who have caused the separation as those who have not. It really is humbling to have to go to someone you honestly believe to have wronged you and say you are sorry and want to be friends again. But our pride is something we should willingly sacrifice for the sake of restoring friendship.

CHAPTER 11
The Way People Are

We become fully caring people when we expand our compassion to include all people.

That's easier to say than to do. Some very good people fail to accomplish it completely. But it doesn't do any good to criticize people for being the way they are.

What you need to do is to allow people to be the way they are and then help them become more than they are.

There's a headline that has achieved a kind of notoriety. Whether it ever really appeared, I do not know. I don't really doubt that it did. It has been used regularly the last quarter of a century as a kind of judgment on people who are turned in on themselves.

The headline that has achieved such notoriety goes: "No Catholics Killed in Oklahoma Tornado."

When it is used it isn't used by newspapermen, at least not by newspapermen who understand what the newspaper business is about. From the time I was a young newspaperman I had city editors telling me to always get the local angle. The same headlines appear often in the daily papers. When there is an airplane crash in some far off country the headlines are likely to read, "Two Americans Among 120 killed in Turkey Crash" or "No Americans killed in Air Tragedy in Egypt." So the notorious Catholic headline wasn't that unusual. It was the natural way newspapermen handle stories, looking for the local angle, tailoring the story to meet the natural interest of their readers.

But it seems to me we need to think about that headline in the way it is used as a kind of an accusation of our parochial attitudes. It is important we think about it, not because it is wrong to ask people to expand their compassion to include all people—we should do that—but because the accusation comes too soon.

It is important that we approach people where they are. It doesn't really do much good if we ask people to be different than they really are without helping them understand why they should be. You may make people feel guilty that way but you aren't going to help them escape from the reason for their guilt.

You have to come to people understanding how they are. The way people are, they can most naturally feel compassion for those who are most like them. Their compassion comes most naturally when the victims of tragedies are their own neighbors and their own friends. Everyone understands that. But when the victims of tragedies are not friends and neighbors, compassion comes more easily when people can identify with the victims.

When there is an airplane crash in Turkey the compassion comes more easily for the two Americans who are killed than for the 118 who are foreigners. If 15 people are killed on the way to a Methodist Church picnic then Methodists have a greater sense of compassion than Catholics will have, just as if those killed had been on their way to a Catholic picnic the compassion felt by Catholics would be greater than that felt by Methodists.

That is one of the reasons that White people have been so slow in their recognition of the injustices suffered by Black people. White people simply don't have a sense of identification with Black people; they are different and so what happens to them doesn't have the same immediacy as what happens to those who are like them.

I hope you understand I'm not saying all of this is the way it should be. It isn't; it very much isn't the way things should be. But that's the way things are and you need to understand things the way they are before you can hope to change them.

It's no good to try to make people feel guilty about the way they are. First of all, people don't know why they are the way they are. When you accuse them of something they don't really understand then you force them into defense of the way they are.

What you must do is not to make people feel guilty about the way they are but rather to help them expand their consciousness of others, to move out from the narrowness of what they are to a broader compassion that embraces all people.

I think that is what has been happening among us. The mobility of people has expanded our concern. Northerners have moved to the South, Southerners have moved to the North, and the old inflexible attitudes have changed with them.

Television has expanded our consciousness. We are suddenly made neighbors with people everywhere in the world. We could have read of starvation in the Sub-Sahara and it might never have reached our consciousness. We might have been sorry that people were suffering and even given a contribution to help those far off suffering people. But now people who are suffering come into our living rooms; we see the staring desperate faces, the children with swollen bellies and pencil-thin arms there before us.

Once White people knew Black people almost only in caricature. We may have known some Black people as friends but they were more friends than Black people. What we saw in the movies was a parody that we accepted as reality: the Black man who was so scared his kinky hair stood on end and his face turned white in fright; the lazy Black man who shuffled when he walked and said, "Yassuh, yassuh."

But it was television and a changed news media that jarred us to understanding. It was courageous Black men and Black women who stood firm for their own rights who forced us to an understanding that we are not different people but the same people. We are and should be shamed by how long it has taken us; we can and should be shamed that there are still people who have not come to understanding.

Even for them, though, the answer is in expanded consciousness. They must be brought to understanding that the only way we can be truly human is to care for all who are human.

CHAPTER 12

The Death of a Child

I think I never realized how many children die, how often boys and girls are taken from life just as it is beginning for them.

But the letters I receive tell me what a common experience this is.

He wanted to talk. He had to talk. He said he hadn't been able to talk to anyone about it. He came to me because he had heard my radio program. He didn't know me, I didn't know him.

He hadn't been able to talk to his wife. He belonged to no church, so he had not had a clergyman to help him. But he had to talk.

He had built a swing for his little four-year-old daughter. He was swinging her.

"Make me go higher, Daddy," she said. He pushed her. "Higher, Daddy, higher."

He gave a big push, the swing went high, then at the top the rope snapped. The little girl was thrown out, she struck against another tree. She was already dead when he reached her.

He wept uncontrollably. She was his only child, he loved her so much, and she was dead because of him.

Of all the tragedies of life the death of a child is the one that I know least well how to handle. The death of any child is so great a sorrow that there seem to be no words to help. But the death of a child when the father has the sense of being responsible for that death is a tragedy that was beyond any words from me.

So I wept with him. I know words to say when there is death, words that I believe have truth, but I didn't know any words to say to that father.

I suppose there were words I said: it was just an accident; there was no reason for him to feel guilt; he was acting in love; nothing words really. All I could really offer him were the tears I shed with him. Maybe that was the best thing I could offer. I wept because I could not help but weep.

I don't know how long we talked, more than an hour surely. He talked about his little girl, about the sweetness of her and the loveliness of her.

He talked of his wife, how she had comforted him, how no one had blamed him—only that he could not help but blame himself.

As he talked his weeping stopped. He smiled as he talked of his little girl; he even laughed about some of the cute things she had said.

Then he was quiet. He looked at me, his face filled with longing for assurance. "You do believe in Heaven, don't you?" I said, "I do, I do very much." "You do believe some day we'll be with Judy in Heaven, don't you?" I said, "I am certain of it."

"I've never thought much about religion," he said. "I went to Sunday School when I was a little boy; it's been a long time ago."

He looked at me, his eyes fixed on my eyes, "You do believe Judy is in Heaven, don't you?"

I said again that I did.

When he stood to leave he was smiling, "Thank you, you've helped me so much." He reached out for my hand and he pressed it hard. He left and I never saw him again.

He had been helped. I know that. He had been helped by talking about the sadness that burdened him, by the sense of guilt that was too much to bear.

I thought at first I hadn't really helped him. I had wanted to help him. I had wanted to say words that would comfort him but I didn't know the words.

Later I began to understand the way I may have helped him. I had helped him by sharing his grief. If it had been my choice I would have been the counselor, the one who spoke the right words, the one who offered calm words of comfort, but I didn't know how to do that. I wept because I was overwhelmed by the sadness of what had happened.

I suppose that counseling should be more than that and yet I think it may be there are times when all we can do is share the grief of those who come to us.

I think, too, I was able to share my faith with him. I do believe in the reality of Heaven. I wasn't just saying this to comfort him, I said it because I believe it. I think that if I'd said it only because he wanted me to say it, only because it would comfort him, he would have known it. I said it because I believe it and he borrowed from my faith and he knew it too.

It was not the first time I'd talked with parents of a child who had died; I have talked with others since.

When I say I do not know what to say I do not mean there is nothing that can be said. But it is simply a sadness that overwhelms me.

There are tragedies in our lives that we simply have to live with as long as we live. I think the death of a child must be one of these.

Dwight Eisenhower said in his last years that the death of his son at four was a sadness that never left him. I think that must be the way that it is.

There are many sadnesses we always carry with us. Time heals our wounds, we are told, but that really isn't true. The passing of time may take away some of the sharpness of the pain but the wounds remain. We do not live by forgetting; we live by learning to live with our wounds.

CHAPTER 13

When Something Bad Happens

Some people thrive under adversity. Many people collapse under it.

There was a letter not long ago from a woman who had lost her husband, discovered his business was in shambles and was left literally destitute with a family to support.

But she did something about it; took over the business; made it work; reared and educated her children.

Yet there have been other letters from people who are not able to recover from the misfortunes of life.

There's no way we're going to go through life without some unfortunate things happening to us.

That's important because if you don't understand this then you can allow your misfortunes to burden you throughout your entire life. "Why me?" That's the cry of those who have suffered misfortune. A better question would be, "Why not me?"

With all the misfortune there is in the world then why shouldn't we expect we'd get our share of it? If we realize that we're going to get our share of bad breaks then we'll be better able to handle them when they come along. When we're knocked down then we can get up, brush ourselves off, and go on.

I learned most about how disastrous it is to allow your misfortune to become a burden through all your life from Ellen. I tried but I never was able to help her.

The first time I met her, her appearance startled me. She was so thin that the skin of her face was pulled paper taut against the bones of her face.

In the months that followed we became friends and I came to know the circumstances that had brought her to a situation that threatened her life.

She had been a beautiful young girl. I saw the photographs of Ellen as she was and she was beautiful. She was talented; played the lead in Little Theater productions; was so good that there were those who said she had a future as a professional.

A man who did profiles of film stars for the *Saturday Evening Post* saw her and was impressed. He talked with friends at Metro-Goldwyn-Mayer. It was arranged that she would have a screen test for MGM; she was to go to New York City.

Ellen was on the top of the world. She had confidence in herself. Everything was going right for her. She bought a new wardrobe for the appointment in New York.

As she left home, she reached down to give a farewell embrace to her pet dog. He bounced around and he scratched her face. It was just a small scratch and she thought that makeup could cover it.

When she arrived in New York, her luggage had been misplaced. She waited and it still couldn't be found. They took the name of her hotel and said they'd deliver it as soon as it was found.

By now she had begun to panic. Everything was going wrong. The man who had arranged her appointment with the people at MGM met her, took her to the hotel, told her everything would be all right.

But the scratch on her face began to redden; there was an infection. Her face was swollen, partly from the infection, partly from her tears.

The day for the appointment came. The luggage had not arrived; she said she couldn't meet the MGM people. They were understanding. The film official had to go back to Los Angeles but he said that another date could be set for the meeting.

The luggage finally arrived but it was too late. She returned home, totally defeated. Everything had gone wrong. She stayed at home, refused to see friends. The infection had passed but the wound of her spirit, her self confidence, remained.

A couple of months later she discovered she had gained considerable weight; her only comfort had been in eating. Her father had been an obese man; it had contributed to his early death. She had always had a fear that she might, too, become obese. So she placed herself on a starvation diet.

When I met her it was more than ten years after that misfortune in New York, but it was still the dominating influence in her life. Her fear that she might become excessively heavy had led to such dieting that her appearance was startling. You would think that just by looking into the mirror she would realize this. But she did not.

Her mother, a widow, doted on her only child. When I came to know them they both told me, again and again, of the misfortune Ellen had experienced and it was as if they were talking about something that had happened a week before.

When I suggested that Ellen needed psychiatric help they were at first offended. Then, because we became friends, it was agreed that they would go to a psychiatrist friend of mine.

He found the situation almost impossible. Finally he was fighting to save Ellen's life, arranging for vitamin shots, trying to get her to eat sensibly.

A few months later Ellen died, died of starvation although her circumstances were comfortable. Her mother told me the last thing she talked about was the way things had gone that week in New York City.

Ellen's case was unusual; she had allowed her temporary misfortune to dominate the rest of her life, finally allowed it to destroy her life.

It could have been so different. The writer who had arranged her opportunity said that she could have had the test later. He said there was no doubt in his mind she had the talent to succeed and she really was a beautiful girl. But she never learned to handle the bad break.

If Ellen's inability to handle her misfortune was extreme, I've known many others who have carried the effects of misfortune though all their lives.

But there are others who use their misfortunes, who become stronger because of them. It not only happens but the truth is that most people who achieve success in life do so despite misfortune. Often the truth is that they achieve success because of their misfortune.

It seems to me the difference in response comes from the expectations. If you expect that your life will be free from difficulties, that everything that happens is going to be what you want to happen, then when the inevitable misfortune comes in your life you'll see it as kind of personal attack from the fates.

But if you understand that bad breaks are as likely in your life as good breaks, if your expectation is that along the way things aren't always going to be exactly as you want them to be, then you're not surprised when you get your share of misfortune.

There are tragedies in life. Some may be almost more than you can handle. But you can handle them because you must. Life must go on, so you go on. You may carry the wounds with you but you must go on.

What you need to understand is the question you must ask. It isn't, "Why me?" It is, understanding there are tragedies in life: "Why not me?" If others suffer misfortunes, if others are given tragedy in their lives, then it should not surprise you that there will be misfortunes and tragedies in your life, too.

If you accept the truth that living means you'll encounter some things in your life that are not what you want then you'll be able to handle your misfortune, even be strengthened by it—and build your life on it.

CHAPTER 14

Everyone's Different,
Everyone's the Same

Not all of my mail comes from people with problems. Some of it comes from people who have opinions about other people.

What I've discovered is that most people who criticize other people strongly are really upset because other people aren't like themselves.

There are two things you need to understand about people—they seem to be contradictory but they are not. Everyone is different and everyone is the same.

Let's talk about the way people are the same first of all. One of the problems people have, and this is especially true among young people, is that they believe their problems are unique. They aren't certain of themselves; they have feelings of inadequacy; they don't like the sound of their name; they think their eyes are too small or their noses too large; they think other people don't really like them; they are concerned about their own faults.

In contrast, they see others with confidence and poise, others who are fully in control in all situations, others who have names that have character, others who are beautiful or handsome, others who are universally admired and loved, others who simply have no faults.

But the truth is that those other people they see as

having all the qualities they wish they had probably have the same doubts, the same uncertainties, as have the people who envy them.

When I was a young newspaperman, I was discovered to have a facility as an interviewer and so I was assigned to do stories on the celebrities who came to the city. It turned out to be a revelation for me. I discovered that people who were famous, who had achieved great success in life, were just people, very much like all the other people I'd known.

I think I understood this best many years later when I was invited to the home of Josephus Daniels (the secretary of the Navy during World War I and one of the South's most important publishers), for a press conference with Henry Wallace, then a former vice president and later to be an unsuccessful third party candidate for the presidency in the 1948 election.

The newspaper people who had been invited were almost entirely antagonistic to Mr. Wallace. They were conservatives and Henry Wallace was a political figure that conservatives almost despised.

He was a man of pleasant appearance; he had a smile that lighted up his entire face; he seemed to be poised and self-confident.

Then the newspaper people started in on him. Their questions were angry, accusing questions. Whatever he answered there was someone to come back with another question that challenged the answer.

I had long before become used to the fact that famous people were very much like other people but what happened astonished me. Here was a man who had been vice president of the United States, who was known throughout all the world, and he literally collapsed before the attacks that were launched against him.

He didn't become angry, although he could have justly become angry. He just seemed to lose all spirit; there was almost a desperation in the way he retreated before the attacks; the smile vanished and a great sadness replaced it; there was no poise, no self confidence; he visibly flinched at the show of animosity against him.

Finally I could stand it no longer. I rushed in with a question, I forget what it was, that was friendly, that allowed him to regain his poise and give a response that was positive and not a response to an accusation.

It was not that I was a particular admirer of Henry Wallace, I had many reservations about his position on many things, but what distressed me so much that I had to come to his aid, was that he was a human being under attack.

When the press conference was over Mr. Wallace came directly to me. I mentioned a mutual friend, Father Maurice Sheehy, a priest of the Archdiocese of Dubuque who was then a Navy chaplain.

He talked eagerly to me about his admiration for Father Sheehy, went on to talk about how the papal encyclicals on social justice had helped form his ideas. There were other people who were waiting to talk with him but he stayed with me, talking with animation about things he found of value in the Catholic Church. I do not doubt that he was sincere in what he was saying but I understood why he stayed with me. He had found in me a friend when others around him were his enemies.

He was, just as you and I are, someone who could not endure bitterness and animosity. He was a man of international importance but like us all, he needed support and friendship.

When I began interviewing people who were celebrities, I had an awe of the famous. They were certainly people above the common run. But when I interviewed an author whose books were best sellers and whose latest book was a Book-of-the-Month selection, I discovered he was bitter because he thought other authors were copying his style.

I interviewed a famed Hollywood comedian, whom I had admired from my boyhood, and while he was gracious to me I was disillusioned by the way he treated his Japanese servant, humiliating him before me.

I was only six years from afternoons at the old Colonial cinema but I found one of my western heroes was an arrogant stuffed shirt, a far greater admirer of himself than I had been when he was one of my heroes. An executive for one of the nation's largest corporations appalled me by his evident lack of concern for people.

I learned by experience that people are really the same, that fame doesn't really change the way people are and the way people are is that they all have weaknesses, they all have faults.

I wouldn't want to give the idea that all celebrities

disillusioned me. Soon after I'd interviewed the cow-
boy hero who turned out to be so overly-impressed
with himself, I met another of my boyhood heroes,
Tim McCoy. He was pleasant, helpful, friendly, but
what pleased me most of all was that he seemed so
much like other people I had known and admired back
home. The character actor, Andy Devine, pleased me
when during our interview the time came for his
telephone call to his wife and I recognized him as not a
celebrity but a husband who loved and cared about his
wife.

But saying that celebrities are really just like other
people isn't really going to be very helpful to people
who are unsure of themselves because they believe they
have inadequacies that others do not have. After all,
celebrities are a group apart. Realizing they may be
just like other people doesn't help people who never
have felt they were in competition with celebrities but
with other kids in school or other people on the job.

There's something I've learned about this through
reunions of my high school graduation class.

I had written a reminiscence of our school days in
which I had said that we all considered one of the girls
in our class the prettiest of all. She came to talk to me.
"Was that really true?" she asked, and I said that it
was. "That's strange," she said. "I always worried
about my appearance. I thought my nose was too
large, I didn't like my eyes."

There was a boy in our class, handsome, possessed
of a poise unusual in young people, the star athlete in

our school. When we met years later he talked of the insecurity he felt in high school. "I always felt other people looked down on me," he said. "My dad drank too much and he'd come to the games drunk and everyone looked at him. I thought people laughed at me, too."

I had never known anything about it at all; even if I had, I would have certainly not thought any less of the son because of the actions of his father.

But I understood then what I had not understood: the most poised young man in our class, the one who exuded self-confidence, had all along been worried and unsure of himself.

People come to me often who have feelings of insecurity about themselves. What they need to understand is that they are not alone, that other people have the same feelings of insecurity, the same feelings of inadequacy.

Knowing this doesn't necessarily solve the problem but it at least puts it in proper context. What we feel about ourselves is not unique, we share the same feelings with others. Knowing that people are really the same in so many different ways can help us in handling our problems.

When you understand that in so many ways we are all the same, then you are on the way to understanding how you can escape the burden of your concern about yourself.

The reason people have this problem of concern about themselves is that they have made themselves

the center of the universe. If they are concerned about
the size of their nose or their eyes or the set of their
ears, the truth is that nobody else really notices or
cares. We may in self-introspection see ourselves in
parts; other people see us as whole. Some of the most
beautiful women and handsome men I've ever known
were people whose individual features would surely
have not met classical standards. But other people
don't see individual features, they see the person
as whole.

Because in a kind of natural way we make ourselves
the centers of our own universe, we see in ourselves
inadequacies that simply do not exist in reality.

When we understand that other people share the
same feelings of inadequacy and insecurity, then our
own situation loses its uniqueness.

Maturity comes when we stop thinking about ourselves and start thinking about other people. We are
mature when we start caring about other people more
than we care about ourselves. We all of us share in so
many ways, we are the same in so many things, and as
we start caring about others we start solving our own
problems because we come to know they are not only
ours.

But if we must understand we are the same in many
ways, we must realize we are different, too. We must
not only recognize that we are different but we must
respect the difference.

If we are slow to anger then when we see someone
who loses his temper easily we think he does not have

control over himself. If our temper is aroused easily when we see someone who never seems to become angry about anything, we think he has no spirit.

I knew a very good person who easily became angry at things. A drawer that stuck could bring a kick to the cabinet; a five-iron drive that sailed the ball over the green was followed by a club thrown in frustration.

There is no way a thing could ever make me angry; to kick an object that didn't work or throw a club after a bad shot are simply impossible for me. But not because I'm somehow superior, it is simply not in my nature, not a part of my temperament. For my friend it is very much a part of his nature, a part of his temperament.

There are people who talk a great deal; there are people who do not talk much at all. There are people who seek to be the center of attention; there are people who avoid being the center of attention.

We must learn to accept people as they are and to recognize that they are different.

I'm not suggesting that we must excuse everything in other people by simply saying they are different. There are some who say that anti-social behavior and even crime can be excused because those who act in an anti-social manner or commit crimes are victims of factors of heredity or environment. People have a responsibility to act with justice towards other persons and while sometimes the tendency towards wrong actions may be explained by heredity and environment, it cannot become an excuse.

What I'm talking about is the ways people differ from the norms we experience in ourselves. We all too often judge people simply because they aren't just like us.

We are different; you and I are different, too. We must accept the way we are different, allow people to be the way they are and even accept the possibility that the way they are different from us may be better than the way we are.

CHAPTER 15

That's the Way It Is

Everyone has some crosses to bear. But what makes the crosses harder to bear is that we have trouble getting used to them.

But our crosses were fitted to our own shoulders and if we are to live satisfactorily and happily, somewhere along the way we have to get used to them.

A lot of people run into trouble because they don't accept the problems they have.

You are what you are, you have what you have—that's the way it is.

A great many of the letters I receive come from people who are troubled with chronic health problems. Problems of health can be burdensome but you will find them a whole lot more burdensome if you worry about them.

People learn they have high blood pressure or that they are diabetics and they worry about it. They stop living in confidence and start living in fear. That's just going to make the problem worse.

What you've got to learn to do is simply to say to yourself, that's the way it is, and go on living. You take whatever medication can help you; you follow what ever new rules of care and diet are required; and then you forget it.

I can speak with some confidence about things like this because I am a diabetic and I have high blood pressure. I didn't start out with them but I have them now and that's simply the way it is. I do what the doctor tells me I should do but I don't think about them any more than I think about the color of my hair or the color of my eyes.

Now I've known people who, when they learned they were diabetics or had high blood pressure, became invalids. They became so concerned about their health that living for them really stopped. They didn't just have disabilities, they let their disabilities have them.

One of the most wonderful human beings I've ever known was a lady named Kathleen Crowe. She was arthritic, so much so that for the last 30 years of her life she was never out of bed. But except for the fact that she had to spend a good part of her life in bed, she lived as fully as anyone I've ever known.

She lived her life from where she was. She didn't think about her handicap (although perhaps she had to when the pain got too great) but she accepted it as the way she was and went on from there.

Since she couldn't go to other people, other people came to her. They didn't come as visitors to a sick and disabled person, though, they came to her for the counsel she could offer.

People came to her with their problems. She helped them and they told other people. Young people especially came to her for advice.

She could have given in to her disability but she didn't. She turned herself to other people, forgot her own troubles as much as the pain would allow her to do so, and lived usefully.

The beginning of this is in the acceptance of problems you have, simply admitting to yourself that this is the way it is, and then forgetting yourself by turning yourself towards others.

Nadine and Sallie Woods have been doing that as long as I have known them. They have muscular dystrophy. Their sister, Dell, died of muscular dystrophy and both Sallie and Nadine have been confined to wheelchairs since they were teenagers.

But what good they have done! They started a foundation to battle the illness that incapcitated them, raised hundreds of thousands of dollars that have gone to medical research.

It was a priest friend who helped them most. "You're going to die some day, all of us are. But don't die of muscular dystrophy, die of love, die doing things for other people."

They both have had to battle not only the muscular disease but many other illnesses that the weakness subjects them to—but they've never really allowed themselves to be invalids.

They wear chest respirators to help their breathing during the day, sleep at night in huge iron lungs like victims of polio used to have to use.

But they keep busy with a variety of things. They keep an active interest in politics; they work on community projects; they move outside themselves to caring for others.

They'd rather not have muscular dystrophy, of course. But they do. That's the way it is and so they start from there and do what they can for others.

And that's what all of us have to do. When we were

born we came into the world with certain characteristics—the color of our skin, the nature of our temperaments, the natural talents we have or don't have—if we are to live happily, we accept ourselves the way we are and start our lives from there.

As years pass, there are other things added. We may not like the things that are added but after we have done what we can to take care of them, we simply have to say to ourselves that's the way it is and go on living.

If we worry about what has been added to the way we are, complain because of it, then we'll probably die of it. But that's foolishness; we shouldn't die of our disabilities; we should die from living—living in love and joy and usefulness.

CHAPTER 16

Getting Through the Night

"The hardest thing for me are the nights. It is then that my loneliness is greatest and my problems seem greatest.

"I long for the morning to come and I hate the nights."

Getting through the night is the hard thing. That's what many people who are old have told me. Why it is I do not know but when people grow older they find it more difficult to sleep.

They wake up in the night. Sleep has escaped them. They are wide awake. Because they know their bodies need the rest they try to go to sleep again but the very effort of trying only seems to accentuate the sleeplessness.

It must be a fairly common experience for so many people have told me it is their problem. There's something I can share with them that helps. It is something that was told to me many years ago by an older woman who had learned the secret from her mother before her.

"Whenever I am awake at night," she said, "I pray for other people. My mother taught me that. She said that when we pray in the middle of the night we may be the only person in town who is praying."

It is important that we always seek to turn our thoughts away from ourselves. It is important that we pray. So we combine the two by using our sleeplessness for prayer for other people.

You are awakened at 3 a.m. There are others in the city who need your prayers. There are people who are desperately ill. There are people who are dying. There are people who are burdened with troubles, people who are overcome by depression. Whether you live in a great city or in a small town there's someone who needs your prayers.

You really may be the only one in town who is praying. Of course, that doesn't mean we can better get the attention of God; He is always open to our prayers, but a part of the way praying is for us is related to how it seems to us, and just the realization that you may be the only one in town who is praying can give you a special sense of nearness to God.

Praying for others has more meaning for you when you think of special people for whom you are praying. You can pray by saying that you are praying for all people but your prayer has a special quality for yourself when it is directed more specifically.

So you say, "Dear God, I pray for someone in this town who is very ill tonight." Or, "Jesus help someone who feels a sense of hopelessness in life." When we pray more specifically we unite ourselves more completely with others.

I don't know if prayers like this are more pleasing to God. I suppose it is if we find in this way of praying a greater sense of love for others.

Some people have trouble composing their own

prayers. That's too bad, because prayer should come from our hearts and not just from our memories. But that's the way some people have learned to pray and if it is easiest for them then that must be all right.

For these people, though, I offer a favorite prayer of mine, composed by St. Augustine. It goes:

"Watch Thou, O Lord, with those who wake or watch or weep tonight, and give Thine angels charge over those who sleep. Tend Thy sick ones, O Lord Christ. Rest Thy weary ones, bless Thy dying ones, soothe Thy suffering ones, pity Thine afflicted ones, shield Thy joyous ones and all for Thy love's sake."

It is a beautiful prayer, one I've loved since first I learned it many years ago, and it is a good one for praying when you have trouble getting through the night.

I said that learning to pray at night when you may be the only one in town who is praying is a secret that may help. It was nearly two years ago I told the people of *Powerhouse* of this and since then I have heard from many of them.

Some write to tell me that praying at night for others has turned out to be the way they find sleep again. One lady wrote that almost as soon as she starts praying for others she falls immediately back to sleep. Many others have had similar experiences.

I can understand that. First of all, it is a turning away from thoughts of self. Our aches and pains grow when we meditate on them and if we are thinking of others then we don't have time for thinking about ourselves. Thinking of others relaxes. When what we are thinking about is how we're going to get back to sleep then we become tense and the sleeplessness is only accentuated. Those are human reasons why praying for others helps the return to sleep but there's nothing wrong in that; things like that are a gift from God—everything doesn't have to be miraculous.

But one crusty old gentleman—I call him crusty because he writes to me often and he writes crustily—said it best: "If praying for others in the middle of the night is supposed to put me back to sleep, let me tell you it doesn't work for me. I don't go to sleep. But that's all right. What bothered me most was the uselessness of being awake. Your way takes care of that. I don't get back to sleep any easier but I don't feel useless any more when I'm awake."

CHAPTER 17

He Sure Could Whistle

"I have a neighbor who is always putting other people down. She finds something to criticize in every one she knows. I don't want to be impolite to her but sometimes I feel like telling her to shut up."

Will Rogers is supposed to have said that he never met a man he did not like. Since liking and disliking is an action of the emotions, I'm not certain I can say that. But what I can say is something very close to it. I've never met a person in whom I was not able to find some good.

I remember the story they told about Mrs. Finnegan, who always had something good to say about everyone. She never missed a wake and when she went she'd stand by the casket, look down on the body of the deceased, and then pronounce a eulogy that listed at great length good qualities she had found in the recently departed.

When a man in town who was by general agreement a thorough reprobate passed on, there was not much sorrow but there was considerable curiosity about how Mrs. Finnegan could possible say anything good about him.

He was a crook and a liar. There was hardly a person in town who had not at one time or another been cheated or deceived by him. He was shiftless and there were those who said he had never done an honest day's work in his life. He was surly in manner and uniformly unpleasant to everyone. He was known to beat his wife, who supported the family by her own labors. His children he treated even worse than his wife—if that were possible.

Mrs. Finnegan dutifully arrived at the funeral home, moved to the viewing room and stood by the casket, looking down at the body of the man who had been the most disliked person in town.

There was silence as those who were there waited to hear what she would say. A few times she started to move her lips, then shook her head and thought a little longer. Finally she shook her head sadly and said, "Well, he sure could whistle."

For most people you don't have to look that hard. There really is some good in everyone.

It is important to look for the good in others, not just for the sake of those in whom you find some good, but for your own sake even more.

People who go around looking for what's bad in people probably won't be disappointed. There are faults in everyone. But the very act of trying to find things to criticize in others does harm to yourself.

But finding the good in others cannot help but make for greater happiness in your own life.

If, in your life, you seek to mine all the possible bad you can find in others then you accumulate only bad; if, in your life, you search for the good in others then what you accumulate is good.

As I write this I realize it sounds trite. I wish I could put it in a more convincing way, offering some psychological explanations. Perhaps someone else can. My only excuse for the triteness is that it really is true.

CHAPTER 18

The Loneliest Loneliness

"I ask your prayers for a young woman in my ward. She has had a difficult time and she cries almost all the time. When she cries I pray for her.

"Sometimes I get the blues because I think no one really cares about me but when I am thinking of her and her troubles then I find caring about what happens to her makes me less concerned about myself."

A letter very close to this came to me from a patient in a mental institution in Illinois. Of all the lonelinesses, the loneliness of the mentally ill is especially painful.

Among the people who write to me often, so that I keep close to their lives, are three who are patients in mental institutions. One man writes to ask that I encourage prayers to Our Lady of Mental Peace. A woman writes to tell me of others in the hospital, detailing their particular problems and asking prayers for them.

The third letter-writer comes with a difference. The other two write well-ordered, perfectly coherent letters. I know they are patients in a mental institution only because they have told me so. But the third letter-writer, a young woman, writes letters that are disjointed. Her letters are usually only two or three sentences long but she will try again and again to write a relatively simple word, crossing out each of the tries until she finally gets it right. Her handwriting shows a kind of wandering in her mind; sometimes in mid-word the writing descends far below the line.

I'm glad for all three but it is the young woman's letters that I await most eagerly. Her letters tell me how she is doing. She addresses me by my first name, as do most of the people who write to me, and she will say, "Think I am doing better this week" or "This has been a difficult week, remember me."

I said she is a young woman. I'm not certain how I know that or even if I do know it. Perhaps she told me in an earlier letter that she is young. I think of her as a young woman, though.

The reason I have a special concern for this woman is that her letters virtually shout her loneliness. The other two have seemed to make some adjustment to their environment; both have moved away from their own selves to concern for other people. But the third letter-writer seems to be desperately lonely, wanting and needing someone to share her battle for recovery.

When I think of all the lonelinesses in the world I can only conclude that the mentally ill have what may be the greatest loneliness. They are, first of all, isolated from those they love, as isolated as inmates of penal institutions.

In the nature of their illness, they are in a sense isolated from their own real selves—a sense of being lost even from the fullness of who they are.

What makes it worse is that so few people understand mental illness. Most people still look on mental illness as if it were somehow disgraceful. People have

a natural sympathy for those afflicted with usual illnesses but they are uncomfortable about the mentally
ill. When someone recovers from another illness, there
is a kind of happy celebration of recovery among
family, friends and neighbors. The recovered mental
patient comes home and is viewed with a kind of
uneasy suspicion; friends unable to understand the
illness are unable to understand the recovery so they
cannot celebrate it with the returned patient.

Loneliness in the mental institution is intensified
because so often family and friends almost completely
abandon them. Why this is I am not certain. A part of
it may be that in not understanding the nature of the
illness they think the patient would not be able to read
the letters they might send. I suppose a part of it is
that people have a kind of feeling of shame about
mental illness, as if the patient has somehow disgraced
family and friends.

I saw the film, *One Flew Over the Cuckoo's Nest,*
and I did not recognize the people. That may be
because of the limits of my own experience but I think,
too, it may be that for dramatic effect the author may
have brought together in an unrepresentative way
many of the more seriously ill.

I know they were not like my friends.

It was more than fifteen years ago that, wanting
somehow to help mental patients, I volunteered to
teach a class in creative writing for the state hospital at
Austin, Texas, where we were living.

The woman who was in charge of the educational

program at the hospital liked the idea. She said she didn't know if there would be much of a response but she was glad for me to try.

So I started a twice-a-week class. The first class had four or five present, the next class was double that, and in the nearly three years that the class continued I sometimes had as many as forty students and more than a hundred attended at one time or another— patients would leave the hospital and so the class would lose members, gain new members.

There were about a dozen men and women who were with the class throughout the whole time.

What the class members did was write whatever they wished, and then bring it to the class. If they were willing, they would read their own writings to the class. If they were too shy to do so, I would read what they had written.

One young man, I'd judge to be about thirty, wrote beautiful poetry. He was not an educated man; he had been in the hospital for six or seven years when I first met him. But he didn't write rhymes, he wrote poetry. I do not feel a competence as a judge of poetry but I knew a man who was competent and he told me how good this man's work was. I was able to get some of his pieces published but he really seemed uninterested in that. He did not read his own poetry but had me read it; he said he liked to hear his own words from someone else, it meant more to him that way.

Another man wrote a continuing serial. There was a program on television in those days called *Rawhide*, about cattle drives, and his serial for our class was inspired by that program.

But the material was completely original. Eventually it became custom for the class to start with his reading of the latest chapter of a cattle drive that went on for more than two years and undoubtedly was the longest cattle drive in history.

He went less for drama than for humor. No one enjoyed the humor more than he enjoyed it himself. As he approached something humorous he worked hard to control his own laughter at what he had written. His laughter was infectious and week after week we all laughed with him.

Sometimes the writings were in the form of short stories, sometimes as essays of remembrance of days long past, sometimes as poetry, sometimes without any form at all.

But what I marvelled at was how completely normal the class was. I had almost no sense of teaching a class of mental patients. They were intelligent men and women; they had a lively interest in what they were doing and what others were doing. They entered into discussions of what had been written. What struck me most was that criticism was always charitable. I don't remember even once any comment concerning another's writing that was designed to hurt.

I have taught college classes where the students did not approach the quality of interest shown by this class of people who were mentally ill.

I am well aware that the very nature of the class

brought students who were unusual. I do not pretend that from this experience I am able to speak with any authority concerning mental patients. But these were patients at a mental institution and these were intelligent, well-mannered and alert men and women. I believe that if I could have moved the class to the classroom at the university where I taught and outside observers had attended the class, those observers would never have imagined that they were mental patients.

I am not competent in the area of psychology but I think the class had therapeutic value. Some of the writing was simply a release; the serialized cattle drive was enjoyed by everyone but the man who wrote it escaped from the hospital every time he wrote his chapters and read them to the class.

But some of the writing was an articulation of the problems of the writers. One young woman wrote what seemed to me to be a very good short story about the end of a marriage because of the wife's infidelity. After class she came to me and said, "That was my own story. I was the woman who was unfaithful to her husband."

I learned after a few weeks that when I came to the class I would be at the hospital for three hours or more. The students came to me after class, just to talk, sometimes about their own problems—but not really very often, more often just to talk, needing to be in contact with someone outside, someone who was a friend.

Jean—the young man who wrote beautiful poetry—

became a special friend. Because he was so talented, I wanted to help him. He was so intelligent, so completely rational, that it seemed wrong for him to be in the hospital.

But he told me he had no hope of leaving. "You do not know me," he said. "There are times I become very violent. It would not be safe to release me." That seemed impossible but when I inquired, I was told that it was true of him.

He was always interested in my family, especially the children. One day we were sitting on one of the benches in the yard outside. "I have a son," he said. "I have not seen him since he was a baby."

I said I had not realized he was married. He said, "I'm not now. She waited for me awhile but then she got a divorce. She married again. I was glad of that. I knew him. He is a good man."

He was silent for awhile.

"That's another reason I must never leave here. It would make it difficult for her and for my son," he said. "I told her she should divorce me and marry again, give the boy a father, because I would never be able to return. If I were to leave I'd want to see her again, I'd want to see my son. It would spoil everything."

Of all the students in the class, I remember Mary best of all. She was an older woman; I'd guess in her late forties. Most of those in the class were much younger.

She started coming in the first weeks I started teaching. The staff was excited about that. They told me she had been at the hospital for many years and in all that time she had shown no interest in anything; she seemed oblivious to anything about her; so far as anyone could remember she had never spoken a word.

She didn't say anything in the class either. She sat in one of the back rows, never responding to anything that went on; she seemed almost not to even be listening. But class after class she was there.

Then one day after class she came forward, walked up to me and pushed a piece of paper into my hand. Somewhere I still have that piece of paper but it is lost in the boxes and file cases. I remember it though.

She had written: "Once I was on a train. It stopped. I looked out the window of the train into the window of a house. There was a mother and father, sitting at a table, their children at the table around them. They were laughing and talking. I cried."

I read it aloud at the next class, said it was beautiful because it was and the others in the class said how beautiful it was and the words warmed her. After the class, members of the class spoke to her, said how much they had liked what she had written.

A few classes later she spoke her first words, wrote other things and finally even read her own pieces. A few months later there was exciting news. She had a job, working outside the hospital, coming back at nights. She still came to the classes though and the change in her was the most satisfying thing that happened in those nearly three years.

The time came that I had to leave Austin and it was a sad moment for us all. I didn't want to talk about it, they didn't want to talk about it, but the day approached when I would be going away.

Then the dozen or so members of the class who had been with the class through all the time did a beautiful thing for me. By chance none of the members of the class were Catholics but they knew I was.

One of the Paulist Fathers at St. Austin's came out to the hospital on Wednesdays to celebrate Mass for the Catholic patients. The members of the class, without telling me they were going to do it, went to Mass together, as their gift to me. They told me about it before the next class and said they had gone to pray for me and my family.

It was Mary, who had been so long silent but became an easy talker, who told me how it all puzzled her. This was in the days before the renewed liturgy and the Paulist priest was an excellent but a quiet man who came to the hospital more out of assignment than wish.

"I know the Catholic Church must be very good," Mary said, "but I couldn't make any sense out of that preacher. He came in, didn't look at anyone, turned his back on everyone and prayed in some language I couldn't understand and he didn't hardly turn around at all until he gave the Catholics a wafer and then he just finished up and left."

When I tell you about my friends at Austin State Hospital my purpose is to make you see them as the wonderful people I came to know and love. I think the great trouble is that those outside simply stop thinking of those in mental hospitals as persons.

People are able to understand other forms of illness, to have compassion for those who are ill, to understand how important it is to those who are ill to have support from those who are well.

But mental illness seems somehow to freeze compassion. Not, I think, because people don't want to have compassion but their lack of understanding of mental illness makes it impossible for them.

I think much that has been written about mental illness—the novels, the plays—creates a false impression. I remember novels that showed an unrelieved horror; I've seen plays that reduce mental patients to eccentric comics.

But what I think is a truth that needs to be understood is that in mental hospitals there are many who are very much like you and me, people, who if you met them, you'd recognize as people who might be your friends and neighbors.

There is a kind of desperate loneliness in their lives, though, and what they need most of all is you. They need their friends to remain their friends, their families to support them, and when they are well enough to return they need to be greeted by people who are happy for them because they are well.

And outside the hospitals there are millions of people who are battling depression, struggling against breakdowns. They need their friends. They don't need them to diagnose their illness, give them talks about cheering up. They just need people who love them, who are concerned about them, who are friends supporting them by just being friends.

CHAPTER 19
Stress Goes with the Territory

There are many stresses in modern life. For that matter, there always have been stresses. We've just learned to talk about their existence.

People who write to me are often people who find their life experiences hard to handle.

There was a letter from a man who lost a job, not because he hadn't done a good job but because the company decided to reorganize and his position was cut out. A woman found her husband's frequent shifts to new locations too difficult for her to take.

Stress is a reality.

There are things you learn that when you think about them apply to other, quite different things—like learning to catch a baseball.

When I was a kid I'd play catch with a grownup cousin who played ball on the town team. He'd burn them in on me and they would sting and my hand would become swollen and red.

He hadn't been intending to burn me out, which was what we called it when some kid threw to you hard as he could. When he saw my hurt hand, he taught me a lesson that kept me from ever getting a swollen hand again.

When you're catching a ball, he told me, there are three things you can do with your glove hand. You can move it a little ahead as you catch it. That's going to add the movement of your hand toward the ball to the velocity of the ball and that's going to really get your hand stinging. Or you can just hold your hand firm and still, taking the full force of the throw, and you'll get a sore hand out of that, too.

But the third way was the way you wanted to do it. As you caught the ball you let your gloved hand go back with the movement of the ball, slowing it down as you caught it by moving your hand with the ball, not a big movement back, almost imperceptible but with the ball.

That's how I learned to catch a baseball without stinging my hand and that's a lesson I think can be applied to other things, including what is called stress.

There's a lot of talk about stress these days. I saw an advertisement for a book the other day that had a big banner head across the top that said, "Stress can kill you." Maybe that's true, I didn't buy the book so I didn't read what it had to say.

But I've read a lot of articles on the subject and they said there's more stress than ever these days, that what people had to do was get out of stress situations.

The dictionary describes stress as a force that strains or deforms, which I suppose applies especially to the force on materials, but it adds as a definition that it also means mental or physical tension. One article I read listed some of the major stresses human beings face and rated them from 100 down to 10, death of someone you love being 100 and other kinds of crises in life rating on a descending scale.

When I added up all the various kinds of stresses I've encountered one time or another, I came up with such a big total I should have been dead. But I'm not and neither are a lot of people I've known who have run into some stressful situations in life.

It seems to me important that we all understand that stress is a part of living. There's no way we're going to get through life without running into situations that are going to give us physical and mental tensions. They go with the territory; if you are living you're going to have stresses in your life.

That's important to understand because if you think you're not going to run into any stress situations then you're not only fooling yourself, you are setting yourself up for a big surprise when it happens.

If you are wise you'll live with an understanding that along the way there are going to be mental and physical tensions, you keep ready for them and when they come you aren't going to be thrown by them.

It has been my observation that most people can handle adversity in life, probably better than they can handle prosperity.

I knew a couple once, good people, God-fearing, praying people. They had half a dozen children and all the time they had troubles. One of the children died, in an accident, and it tore them up but they survived, better for the hard experience, closer knit as husband and wife, closer as a family.

They never had enough money, they were always running just to catch up, and when they about made it then a refrigerator would go dead or the transmission would fall out of the old car and they'd be running to catch up again.

But they were a beautiful family, the husband and the wife were knitted together by all the problems they had; the children helped because they knew they had to help.

Then the husband switched jobs, got into a line of work where he turned out to be a whiz. He started making money, not just enough to get caught up, but big money and all of a sudden they were wealthy.

They got a whole new set of friends; it was necessary they said because that was the way you made contacts. They were off to Jamaica for winter vacations, got themselves a summer house at the lake. They were prosperous and then just as suddenly everything started unraveling. Adversity they could handle, it pulled them together. Prosperity was too much for them; what the tensions of life had brought together the affluence of life unloosed. The marriage broke up, the children scattered and a beautiful family was no more.

That doesn't have to happen to everyone who gains some sort of affluence, of course, and I'm not suggesting it does. But what I do know is that adversity can, when people handle it with a loving caring for each other, draw people closer.

Of course, the key is in how you handle the stresses you encounter in life. That's where I think learning how to catch a baseball can help you. I don't want to try too hard to make the parallel but I think it's there in a way.

I've known people, and you have, too, who move out ahead to meet the stresses of life. They're certain something bad is going to happen to them so they're always worrying about it. They can't appreciate the good times because they know the bad times are on their way. Because they are expecting trouble they're always rushing out to meet it and when it comes they collide with it out front.

Then there are other people who determine they are going to stand absolutely firm against whatever stresses in life they may encounter. They set their chins, keep a stiff upper lip, stand unbending even when the stresses hit them full force.

But there are others who move with their tensions. If there is reason for grief then they weep. If they get bad breaks then they don't try to deny them or pretend they never happened; they bend with their troubles. They say to themselves, well, that was something we didn't want, something that hurt us, and moving with the stresses they keep out some of the hurt and are ready to go on.

As I said, I didn't want to draw the parallel too precisely, as if all you needed to do was learn how to catch a baseball and after that handle all the problems of life. But there's something there, a hint of an explanation; it has helped me, maybe it could help you.

CHAPTER 20
Learning to Pray

People want to learn to pray. There are, of course, people who do not pray at all. They aren't people who write to me. The people who write to me are praying people but they continually struggle with their prayers—never gain an ease in praying.

While, in my earliest memory, it was my mother who taught me to pray, I remember exactly when it was that I prayed in a real way. I was, I judge, either five or six. We moved a few times in my childhood and knowing the years that we moved pinpoints things that happened.

We had just moved to the country outside of the little town of Hamden in the Appalachian southern hills of Ohio. One room in the little house became the spare room. There it was that mother had left the big picture of Christ the Good Shepherd, not having found the place yet to hang it. It was a favorite picture of mine and when I was very little I used to lie on the floor beneath where it was hung in the other house and just look at it.

On this particular day I was sad. A kitten I'd been given had disappeared. Its name was Black Tail; it was mostly white with a black tail, and it had simply disappeared. I felt as if I wanted to pray for my lost kitten and it seemed to me I could do it better if I looked at the big picture of Jesus as I prayed.

There was no order in the spare room, things were

just stacked there, and the picture of the Good
Shepherd was sitting on the floor. I sat down beside it
and said a prayer which asked that wherever Black
Tail might be, he would be all right.

But then I started thinking of Jesus and of God and
I began to pray, not formal prayers (for besides "Now I
lay me down to sleep . . ." I think I knew no other
prayers) but the kind of prayer that simply thinks
about God, that murmurs love for God at times, but
mostly just keeps the thought of God.

It was the first time I had prayed with a sense of the
presence of God. I had prayed before, words that I
meant, but words directed to God as someone
distant—so distant that when I thought of him it was
like thinking of the stars. But that day, for the first
time, I had a sense of his presence; I came not as a
stranger but to someone close to me who would listen
to my words and sense my thoughts, with whom I
could sit never saying a word and be praying.

I suppose the child psychologists would say that a
child of five or six could not think abstractly but I only
know that this was what I experienced that day, and
not with any kind of sense of the unusual; rather it was
a feeling of naturalness I recall.

From that day I have always prayed and in the same
manner. In the years since I've become a Catholic,
particularly in these last two or three years since the
prayer group called the *Powerhouse of Prayer* began,
I've had hundreds of people who have talked to me or
written to me about prayer.

What I was surprised to discover was that there are

many people, prayerful people, who simply either feel incapable of praying in a kind of conversational style or simply have no concept of what that kind of prayer might be.

Many people write to me to say they pray for those who ask for their prayers and then add a decade of the rosary or perhaps five Our Fathers and five Hail Marys.

Once when I was talking to a priest about prayer as I know it, I said I did not pray formally. After he had gone I got to thinking about what I had said and realized I had not really told the truth, for what I had said would indicate that I somehow did not accept formal prayers.

That isn't true. When I became a Catholic I learned to love the rosary. How many years it has been I'm not certain but I have not missed saying the rosary at least once every day for many years and the number of rosaries I've said far exceeds the number of days I have been a Catholic. There are other prayers that have set forms I have said and do say often. So it is not true that I do not say formal prayers.

And yet that is not the kind of praying that is most meaningful and even when I say formal prayers there is a sense of informality in the saying of them—the rosary has always been for me not so much a saying of prayers as a kind of sustained meditation. Since it is a placing of myself in a kind of closeness to Christ, allowing me to be with him and his Blessed Mother in a kind of re-experiencing of the mysteries, it has a kind of informality about it.

While I would not do anything to disturb those good people who are able to conceive of prayer only in the terms of saying a decade of the rosary for someone's intentions, it does seem to me that they would find a much more satisfying experience if they at times simply carried on a conversation with God.

I've tried to explain what I mean and letters I receive tell me that many learn to do this for the first time and find a new closeness to God in doing so.

But even conversation doesn't exactly describe what I am talking about because it suggests that in praying you must be saying something. The very most important part of prayer is without words at all: simply placing yourself in an awareness of the presence of God is prayer.

I know I'm not very good at explaining this because when I've tried to explain it I've been asked if this means you continue a meditation, thinking of the wonder of God. It may be that there may come some thoughts like this but that is not what I'm describing either. The thoughts might not even be directly of God; they might be of problems I face, although not trying to think them out, simply allowing them to pass through my mind. Or there might not be any thoughts at all.

Sometimes, whether you would call it meditation or not, I do not know, I simply place myself in some other place in the world. If I have read that this or that public figure is facing a great decision, I simply think of that person at that moment, wherever that person may be, my mind placing itself where that person is, and then, gaining a mental image, ask God to give that person special help.

In this kind of prayer I open myself to the realization that things are happening everywhere in the world at that very moment, that if there are people suffering from some natural disaster or from starvation their suffering is at that very moment and I bring to my mind these people as they are at that moment and ask God to help them.

When I write this it sounds much more planned than it really is; I don't think beforehand that today I am going to think of and pray for this or that, making a list, but rather simply in the opening of my mind so that what happens comes naturally.

It is true, I think, that if you are to place yourself in the presence of God it follows you have placed yourself in the presence of all people, for all people are forever in the mind of God.

When I have tried to explain this to others I am sometimes asked if by keeping silence, thinking of God, there come answers from God. I've heard it said that we should not only pray but that we should keep silent and listen to God.

It would be nice if I could say, yes, listen to God and He will speak to you but that's not the way I have experienced it. Sometimes in silent prayer, I suppose, there comes unexpected clarity concerning what I should do. That might be God speaking to me, although I've never really thought of it in that way. What surprises me is that when something is clarified for me unexpectedly, it is rarely ever something I was even thinking about. I've never had any expectation that if I just keep quiet God is going to somehow speak to me—that just has nothing to do with the kind of prayer and meditation I'm talking about.

As a matter of fact, it's my experience that when I do have a kind of certainty that God is acting in my life, it has always been apart from any time of prayer and usually in ways that are not at all as I planned them.

If there are those who read this who are better trained in theology than I am, and that would not be difficult, I suppose some might object that in speaking of prayer I do not show more precision concerning prayer to God the Father, God the Son and God the Holy Spirit. This may be an ignorance on my part but for me the unity of the Holy Trinity is such a reality that when I pray, although I may think of each person of the Trinity, and do in my meditations, it is the unity of the Trinity that moves my mind so that when I think of the presence of God it is as the Trinity.

Because what I am trying to convey is not something I articulate but experience, I always wind up any discussion of it with a realization I don't do very well in explaining what I mean.

But to simplify (as I have tried to do for those who come to me and have found many who do understand what I am trying to say), simply try to think of God often through the day. Because if we are in the world there are things we must be about doing; it is not possible to spend the day in meditation.

So you can accomplish this simply by thinking of

God from time to time, saying a quick prayer, "My God, I love You" or "Jesus, help me to be as you wish me to be." Because most people have an awareness of time, I suggested to *Powerhouse* people they might on the hour or the half hour, give a quick thought to God and say a prayer. Many have written to say they have done this but I do not do it myself because when I work I have no awarenss of time; yet in every work there are little pauses when this is possible.

And to help in finding a different kind of praying I suggest that people pray as if they are simply talking to one they love. "Dear Father, you know my neighbor, John, has been out of work for a long time and he's depressed about it. Please help him."

And I urge people to pray more for others than they pray for themselves. In *Powerhouse,* where everyone is praying for everyone else the people have a sense of having others pray for them and so they feel no necessity to pray so much for themselves.

And people who all their lives have been praying say how much better they feel about praying for others than praying for themselves.

That I think is a real understanding of prayer, not as a means for getting what you want, but as a way to embrace all people. If you truly come into the presence of God (and you always are in the presence of God— you need only to come to a realization you are), then you are at the same time in the presence of all people, for all people are forever in the mind of God.

CHAPTER 21

Go Ahead, Feel Sorry for Yourself

I have observed that people often set roles for themselves and, finding themselves unable to fulfill their own expectations, are saddened by it.

But the fault is in our expectations, the role playing we set for ourselves, and the solution is a natural one.

There was a letter from a woman who said she felt guilty because she felt sorry for herself. She told me of all the sadnesses that had come into her life and they were great.

She said she tried to think of others, she tried to think of the blessings in her life, but she kept coming back to feeling sorry for herself. It bothered her because it wasn't the way she wanted to be and she thought it was wrong of her.

I told her to enjoy herself, go ahead and feel sorry for herself and not to feel any sense of guilt about it at all. She had reason to feel sorry for herself and no reason at all that she shouldn't.

It really is best not to feel sorry for yourself, to turn your thoughts towards others, to thank God for your blessings and forget your misfortunes.

But not everybody can do that. I takes a special grace to do it. So if you really just have to feel sorry for yourself then you might as well go ahead and do it.

Chances are doing it is the only way you are ever

going to get over doing it. It wasn't long after that I received another letter from the same woman.

She had taken my advice. She had felt sorry for herself. She had wept over all the sadnesses that had come into her life. She had done it with no sense of guilt in doing it. And after doing it, she felt better and she was starting to move away from feeling sorry for herself.

The gift of tears is a wonderful gift. We shouldn't be afraid of using that gift.

There's really nothing sadder than to see someone resisting tears, as if to cry would show some lack of courage or of faith. So some simply bear their sadnesses, jaws clenched, unwilling to give in to sorrow or self-pity.

To continue in sadness or self-pity would be wrong, not because it is something to feel guilty about but because it is not good for us. While we live we are called to live as joyfully as we can, as usefully as we can; the very health of our body and mind depends on this.

But for many people, probably most people, the only way to reach joyfulness in life is through some valleys of sorrow. If you want to weep then weep. If you want to feel sorry for yourself then feel sorry for yourself. Don't stay there—but then you won't; the purpose of the gift of tears is a cleansing one and its use will bring you to joy, perhaps a bittersweet joy, for we must not expect the sorrows in our life to disappear but they can become a part of the gentle memories that become our new joy.

CHAPTER 22
If I Only

There's a letter I'll receive next week. I know I will because it is a letter that comes to me so often. The details differ but the theme is always the same:

"A close friend of mine and her husband were killed in an automobile accident last month. The sorrow I have over their deaths is great but even greater is the sorrow I have because I realize I never told them how much I appreciated their friendship, how much I loved them."

Or sometimes it is of the family:

"My mother died not long ago. I miss her but what bothers me is I never got around to telling her I loved her. She knew I'm sure but I never said the words and it hurts me I didn't."

I think by my own experience this must reflect one of the most common of all situations that can be found among people.

I'd guess the most common of the burdens people bear in their hearts is that of regret, the regret not for something they have done but for what they have failed to do.

It is so common there are probably none who have not experienced it. It is the regret we have when death takes a friend unexpectedly and we wish we had let that person know of our love and appreciation.

"If only I had told him how much I appreciated all he did." "If only I had told her how much I appreciated her friendship. "If only I had thanked them for all the things they did for me."

You've heard these words. You may have spoken them; almost certainly you have thought them. We all have experienced regret over something we failed to do or say when time ran out. For some people this regret becomes a terrible burden.

But of all the burdens people have this is the one easiest to avoid. All we have to do is to let the people we love know that wc lovc them, the people we appreciate know of our appreciation.

I'm not sure why it is but a great many people have difficulty in telling people they love that they love them or in expressing their appreciation for those who are their friends.

I can think of many possible explanations—an unwillingness to seem sentimental, a sense of privacy about things that are most meaningful. It seems that it most likely may derive from a sense of self-inadequacy, as if admission of love or an expression of appreciation for another somehow diminishes us.

But I don't really know much about things like that and the way doesn't really seem important. What is important is that we must do now what we might wish we had done tomorrow.

When I say we must let those we love know that we love them I am not talking about husbands and wives. But perhaps I should mean them. It is unbelievable to me that a husband and a wife should not tell each other of their love. But I read Ann Landers and so I know it does happen. It is still unbelievable to me, though, and while I've heard the cry of regret from many people, I never heard of it from a wife or a husband.

I'd guess this regret comes most often from the grown children of parents who die unexpectedly. As children we take our parents for granted. They are just always there. When we leave home for school or work or marriage our thoughts are centered on our own selves.

The years pass and we are concerned with our own children. We may sometimes think of our parents with gratitude but we are far more likely to think it than say it.

We must escape all of this. We must tell our parents of our love; parents must tell children of their love. They must do it because love should be expressed, they must do it because those we love need to know we love them, and they must do it because if they do not then surely one day there will come regret.

We all of us know people we appreciate—friends, people we work with, neighbors. But it is easy to keep that appreciation to ourselves and the day may come when we'll regret we never expressed it.

The important thing is to show appreciation for people while they live. You don't have to make a production number of it. Just a simple, "I appreciate you, friend," or a word of praise and gratitude to someone you work with, "You do a good job, you really help me."

I'm not talking about an artificial expression of affection, the kind where people call each other

"Darling"—as a matter of fact, I've never known people like that; I've only seen them in the movies but I don't doubt they exist. Anyhow I'm not talking about that. I'm just talking about ordinary people who hold back the words of praise, affection and love they have in their hearts for others.

What I've learned is that when people do consciously seek to let others know of their appreciation and affection they are happier for doing it; those they tell of their appreciation and affection are happier for the words that have been spoken to them.

The importance of letting those we love know we love them and those we appreciate know we appreciate them is something I learned from my earliest years.

In our family now, as was true in my family when I was a boy, we never leave each other without kissing goodbye; even if we're just going to the grocery store two blocks away, we kiss each other goodbye and say, "I love you."

It was that way when I was a child. We kissed each other goodbye whenever we parted. It was such a natural thing that it was simply a part of our lives. I remember once when I was in high school a classmate had stopped by to go somewhere with me. It was just to go downtown to a movie or maybe to the ballpark. I was going to be back in a couple of hours. But before I left I did as we all did and kissed my father and mother goodbye.

Outside my friend looked at me with amazement. "You mean you kiss your dad and mom goodbye whenever you leave the house," he said. I said of course and he shook his head and said "Jeeze!" I don't remember ever feeling any embarassment about this. If you love someone then it should be natural to express that love. That some have difficulty in doing so probably comes from not being taught to express love openly in childhood.

The expression of appreciation is something you should do equally easily. A long time ago I decided that when I appreciated someone I'd let him know.

I've made a practice of writing letters. We had a mailman at a place I worked who went out of his way to give us good service. I didn't just thank him, I wrote a letter to the postmaster to tell him how much we appreciated this man. The postmaster wrote back to say that in all his twenty-five years in the job he'd never before received a letter of appreciation for one of his carriers.

I've written other letters to employers to express my appreciation for someone whose service I valued. Those who have worked directly under me I've not only thanked personally but made certain those who were over us were told of that appreciation, too.

What I think people should know is that they should be generous with their love, their friendship, their appreciation. People need to be loved, to be appreciated, to feel they are needed. It is miserly to deny them what they need when you have it to give.

I started out by saying to show this generosity is to prevent later regrets. That's true but perhaps there is a little selfishness in this if we do it only to prevent regrets. We should do this because it is right to do it.

But this generosity should extend to all for whom we feel appreciation. We should offer it to all to whom we feel gratitude. We should do it not only to those who might do us some good, (although this, honestly felt, we should do, too) but especially we should do it for those who can never do anything for us at all.

And it is something that should be instilled in children from their childhood. Children who are reared in a family where love is expressed often, where signs of affection are given easily, will find they are able to express their love and gratitude easily when they are older.

There are many things we can do for others, that we should do for others, but nothing we can do for others is more important than letting them know we appreciate them.

CHAPTER 23

The Need for Listeners

She wrote me a long letter, nearly twenty pages. In it she went into all the things that had been bothering her, things that had happened to her, the fears she had, the consolations she found in her life.

When she came to the end of the letter, she wrote almost in surprise.

"I was going to sign my name to this letter but I've decided not to do it. It isn't I'm afraid to let you know who wrote it, it is just I don't need to sign it.

"Just writing to you has gotten many things off my mind and helped me think out some things that were troubling me.

"I suppose I could just throw this letter away, since writing it has helped me so much. But the only reason I wrote it was I knew you would read it. It would be cheating myself if I didn't send it to you.

"But there's no need to bother you with my name. Just say a prayer for me and my family. God will know who I am."

Every mail brings me letters from people who simply need someone to tell about themselves. I have become a listener and I'm blessed by listening.

Tomorrow will bring me more letters. Some of them will be long letters, recitations of problems. They are not directed to me for advice and counsel. I'm really not qualified to offer it; there would be so much more I would have to know to advise them and chances are even then I'd not really be able to give them proper guidance.

But that's not why they have written to me. They have come to me because they need a listener. They need someone who will listen to them. Almost more often than not the letter will not be signed or there will not be an address. They have not come to me for counsel but because they have confidence that I will read what they have written, that I'll try to understand what they are telling me, that I'll say a prayer for them.

And I do read every letter that comes to me; I do listen to what is said; I do feel sorrow for their sorrow, do feel the sense of frustration they have, and do pray for them—and it is not that I think my prayers have some special value or that they think my prayers have some special value but because people just like the idea that someone cares, someone listens to them, someone says a prayer for them.

There is such a need for listeners in the world. We all of us tend to want to talk more than we listen. When we're in a conversation we're likely to be thinking more about what we are going to say when the other person finally stops talking than we are thinking about what the other person is saying.

Almost everyone needs a listener. The letters that come to me are not from people you would think of as lonely. They come often from people who have loving people around them, husbands with good wives and a loving family, wives with good husbands and a loving family, but needing someone to listen to things they cannot really discuss with those they love.

They come to me because I am in a sense anonymous. They come to me because I promise—and it is a promise I keep—that no one else will ever read what they write, that I will never break their confidence in me. They write because they just have to have someone listen to them.

What they gain from this they could probably gain as easily by writing down their thoughts and then throwing the paper away. But most people can't really do that—to do it they must think that someone will read what they have written.

Often at the close of the letter the person who has written will say he or she feels better just getting everything down on paper, that by writing thoughts have been clarified. And then the letter may be signed by only the given name. The need was for a listener.

My own situation is unique. There are probably not many people to whom others will write as a listener. But all of us can be listeners. There are always people looking for someone to listen to them. I know because all my life I've tried to be a listener. When I sense someone wants to talk to me I allow him to talk.

I guess I'm a busy man but I am careful never to give to those who have come to me as a listener any idea of that. A time efficiency man would tell me how many hours I've wasted but I know the time has not been wasted. There may not be much value in the time spent for me—although as a listener you do come to understand human nature better, I think—but what is important is that the one to whom I've listened has been helped.

As a listener, I really don't offer advice. I'm very wary of doing that and people who need listeners don't really come for advice. I just listen, respond where response is absolutely necessary, but say almost nothing myself.

And as a listener I make certain I never retain what I have heard. I've heard people who wondered how a priest who hears confessions could possibly remove from his mind all he had heard and not have his attitudes towards people whose confessions he heard be influenced by what he had heard.

But I understand. I have no priest's seal but no one has ever told me anything in confidence that I have repeated to another person. And one of the reasons this is true—for I suppose I might by accident reveal a confidence—is that while I listen carefully I, by an act of will, do not remember what I've heard.

Some years ago a man of some prominence in his profession came to me as a listener. I listened to him for more than an hour and he thanked me for listening to him.

A year ago our paths crossed unexpectedly. Later when we were alone off to one side of the group to whom he had come to speak, he spoke to me almost in a whisper.

"I hope you will never tell anyone what I told you when last we met," he said. "I've never told anyone else that in all my life."

I said that, of course, I would not. And I won't, because I don't have even the remotest idea of what it was he told me. Whatever his secret was, it is totally safe with me. I wouldn't tell anyone if I remembered it but the truth is I don't remember at all.

There is one danger in being a listener—how dangerous I learned tragically. It is possible for people to come to depend on you as a listener. They don't just need to talk to you, they need to talk to you again and again.

Somehow, as gently as you can, you must discourage this. Not because it uses your time but because it really isn't best for the person who comes to depend on you.

I learned this tragically. He had telephoned me once after hearing a radio broadcast I did. He asked me if I could come to see him and I did.

He repaired violins. Once he had been a concert violinist but after a concert in a city in Texas he was mugged; he resisted, was cut across the hand, the tendons severed. It was his fingering hand and it was left too stiff for him to ever be a concert violinist again.

He loved the violin too much to leave it and he became a repairer of violins. Those who came to him for his work were professionals—once he showed me a violin he was working on that belonged to a man in Paul Whiteman's orchestra.

He was a troubled man and he needed someone to listen to him. I listened and he kept coming back to talk to me again and again. He needed professional help, I knew that. I'm not certain if I ever really talked to him about that; I've thought about it often since and I hope—but that's only for my own peace of mind— that I did tell him that. But if I did it was not likely he would have listened to me. I seldom got a chance to say anything.

I'd been away for two weeks when I came back to the radio station. In my box there were more than a dozen messages. He had called me again and again. The last of the messages was urgent. The one who had taken the message had underlined the words. He had to see me immediately.

I drove out to his home. There was a police car in front of the house and people were standing around in little groups. He had killed himself. What it was he had so urgently needed to talk about I will never know. Whatever it was it became too much for him.

I told myself it was not my fault. I had been away because I had to be away. When I knew he needed me I had gone to him. It was just too late.

Yet in another way I believe I was culpable. I had allowed him to become dependent on me. I should have found some way to get him the professional help he needed. I shouldn't have allowed him to depend so much on me as a listener that without me he could not handle whatever burdened him so much that he took his life.

So even as I say you must, whenever you can, allow yourself to be a listener of those who need you, you must not allow others to become dependent on you. Since this tragic experience I've been careful about this. How you keep it from happening is something you must learn to do by ear; people are different, but even as you become a listener you can find a way to keep those who come to you from being dependent on you.

There is one exception to this and that is of those who are dying. This I learned through the example of a Holy Cross priest named Father Eugene Dore.

Her name was Sophia and she was dying of cancer. She was sad that her life was ending, that she would not live to see her children grow to adulthood but she had a special sadness because while she had always been a Catholic she really knew so little about her own faith.

Because it was what she wanted, Father Dore started her on a course of instruction. She lived for three or four months after she had learned she was dying. Every day of those last months Father Dore came to her, taught her lessons in theology. There was so much she wanted to know.

What that good priest gave her was an advanced course in theology and Sophia became more joyful with every new understanding she received.

He was a busy pastor but almost to the day of her death, as long as she was able to hear his voice, he came to her to teach her the truths she so eagerly wanted to learn. It was her good fortune that she found a priest who understood how important it was to her and did not think it a waste of time to teach someone whose graduation would be in death.

It is not universally true but there are people who realize they are dying who want most of all to have someone listen to them. It was true of Marie. She was the last member of her family. She was not really old but her husband had died before her; there were no children, the only living relative was a cousin in California.

She had left the city where she had lived all of her adult life, where she had friends who would have supported her, to return to the town she had left when she went off to college some forty-five years before. It must have been in the hope she could recapture a long ago happiness but the sadness was that there were almost none who even remembered her.

We met almost by chance—she had been walking, seemed to be ill, so I had stopped to ask if I could help her. She knew me because she had read things I had written.

She was dying but her most desperate need was for someone to listen to her. I saw her every day until finally she had to go to a nursing home in another city. She wanted to talk about her youth, her parents, her husband, her days as a school teacher. She needed someone who would listen as she remembered the past; she was dying of a cancer but she didn't talk about that, it did not seem to be something of major consequence for her; what was important was that she should collect all of her memories and show them to someone else.

It is good to be a listener if the opportunity comes. It is a part of caring.

CHAPTER 24

Good Guys and Bad Guys

"You say our faith should show in our actions towards others.

"I have known people of faith who are very good people, people who help other people. But I've known people who have no faith at all who help other people and who are among the very best people I know."

I know a man—he is no longer young but he was when what I'm going to tell you about him happened—who was shattered the first time he discovered that the real world didn't conform to the world as he had conceived it to be.

He was a fine young man, handsome, pleasant in manner. He was a seminarian in one of the religious orders. Summers he came home to the city in which his parents lived—they had moved there after he entered the seminary so he didn't have friends his own age.

He got a summer job, working at a downtown hotel. The manager of the hotel liked him, gave him a raise, moved him to new responsibilities. When he returned to the seminary the manager and his wife, who had become friends of the young man, told him they would welcome him back the next summer.

That summer came and he had an even better job waiting for him. He became an even closer friend of the manager and his wife and they were like second parents to him.

But then he learned something that almost literally

shattered him. He discovered the manager and his wife, two of his closest friends, were married after divorces and that their divorces had come because they had wanted to end their previous marriages to marry each other.

The young man had been raised strictly in the old style. In his image of the world there were good people and there were evil people. People who divorced and remarried, particularly when their marriages were broken because they had entered into a romantic liason with another person, were evil people.

He came to me on the day of his discovery. What distressed him was that he knew by his own relationship with them what fine people the hotel manager and his wife were. But they were divorced and remarried and in his simple view of life, people who were in that situation couldn't possibly be good people.

He had not come to me for advice, he made that clear when I started to offer it. He had come only to vent his outrage. Not against his friends, the hotel manager and his wife, for he had real affection for them. Not against the position of the Church that marriage is indissoluble, for he believed this is true. His outrage was against his discovery that the neat pattern he had of the world turned out to be not the way the world really is.

The summer vacation had ended when he made his discovery. He had already said his goodbyes to his friends, so he returned to the seminary without seeing them again.

It did not surprise me that at the end of the next school year he left the seminary. What happened to him after that I do not know.

His story is, I suppose, unique. There must not be many people as naive as he was. But there are a great many people who have the same basic problem he had.

They are the people who try to divide the world between the good guys and the bad guys. It just can't be done because there's both good and bad in all of us.

When I was a boy I learned a little verse—I think it was in a book called *Heart Throbs*—that I've remembered all my life. It goes: "There's so much good in the worst of us, and so much bad in the best of us, that it hardly behooves any of us, to talk about the rest of us."

People just can't be categorized as good guys and bad guys. That doesn't mean you should surrender principles, say whatever anyone does is all right.

But it does mean you have to understand that people who might do things you find reprehensible can still be people in whom there are good qualities.

We're all sinners, everyone of us. Some sin more spectacularly than others but we all fall short of being everything we should be. And if there is someone who has never sinned at all, either by commission or omission, then chances are that person sins by being proud of it.

CHAPTER 25
But First Is Love

Dr. Mildred Jefferson, the Black woman doctor who has been the nation's most effective leader of the pro-life movement, was being interviewed on a television program.

A woman in the audience asked if it is right to bring children into the world if parents are unable to offer them advantages.

Dr. Jefferson, who has an ability always to remain calm and pleasant, said that if her parents had decided they had to have the ability to give their children material advantages before they would allow them to be born then she would never have been born.

The saddest of all the rationalizations for abortion comes from those who say they have decided to kill their unborn infants because they could not afford to give them the advantages of life.

Children don't need advantages, they need love. Far more than anything else, children must have love. I've always understood this because I was reared in a family in which there were no great luxuries but where there was always love.

I do not mean I was reared in poverty. That would not be true. My father was a Western Union lineman; he worked hard and he kept us in comfort. Even during the depression, when Dad was working only part-time, we had enough and the lack of money was simply never discussed.

But there were luxuries that we would probably have liked to have had that we didn't have. When I was a little boy there were two things I secretly wanted for Christmas—one of those little cars with pedals and a motion picture projector. But I never asked for them because I knew that these were things I could not have.

My brother and I worked for our spending money. We bought our first dog for fifty cents by churning butter, getting a nickel for doing it, and paying in installments; the dog was not delivered until the last payment was made.

We had paper routes and in the summer we caddied. I sold Cloverine Salve, *Comfort Magazine* and dust caps my Aunt Lydia made, door to door. What we had for ourselves we mostly earned by ourselves. Our first bikes we bought from our own earnings.

Compared to some boys we knew we probably didn't have as many "advantages" but what we had always, the greatest thing we possessed in the world, was the love our parents gave us so generously. I don't remember that we were ever punished. If ever any of us were spanked I do not remember it. But if we did do something we should not have done, the real punishment was in the realization that we had failed our parents, failed the love they had for us.

I saw the need for love later in life, and got a regular job from that need. Soon after I became a Catholic, Bishop Vincent Waters, the bishop of Raleigh, N.C., asked me to come to North Carolina to start his diocesan paper.

Our office was in a building at Nazareth, just outside of Raleigh, a little group of buildings on a hill that had been the project of Father Thomas Price, the co-founder of Maryknoll. It was the site of an orphanage.

The children were well cared for but the busy sisters could not possibly give the many children the kind of love and affection they needed. One day at recess I was out on the grounds and was talking to a little boy. He held up his arms and I picked him up and held him. Another child came up and wanted to be held, too. Soon there was a line of little boys and girls, waiting to be held.

After that it was an everyday job. If the children saw me they'd come running, line up, I'd pick them up, give them a hug and put them down again. Sometimes they'd run to the back of the line, wanting to be held again.

What they needed was love. That's what all children need, love. Don't tell me that children need "advantages," there are parents who give their children all the "advantages" except love. The thing they could give them most easily, they deny them because they don't understand that children don't need things, they need to be loved.

When Chris came into our family, I was scared. Barbara had brought him home. The sisters needed a temporary home for him. His mother, unmarried and very young, had almost completely abandoned him. What scared me was I thought he was going to die. He looked like the children whose photographs you see in stories about starvation. His face and body were emaciated except for a swollen little stomach. His eyes were big and staring.

Barbara said what he needed was love. The prescription was that he should be held, talked to, loved. We took turns. There were four of us. There was Fanny Carr, a Negro woman who helped us and was our friend. There was a wonderful young woman who by tragic circumstance was expecting a child outside of marriage and had come to live with us while she waited for her child.

We called him Christopher. We were never told his real name or the name of his mother. He was to be our child only until he was healthy and adoption could be arranged.

Chris got love. He got love in abundance and it was only a matter of a few weeks before he started filling out, started laughing, was a happy healthy baby. In three months he was the healthiest baby you'd ever hope to see. We gave him food, gave him material sustenance better than he had had before, but that wasn't what made the difference. It was love that he had needed most. He needed arms that held him and voices that made sounds of love.

He was adopted by a good family that had wanted a child to make it a family. A year or two later I met his new parents. They had come to the city. They lived in another town, and they just wanted to thank us. I was introduced to them, they told us the name they had given Chris, but all of this I put out of my mind for I didn't want to know it. It was enough to know Chris had a good home.

I think about him though. He would be in his twenties now, probably through college. Sometimes I wish I'd remembered his name and the name of his parents. I'd like to know how things are going with him. But I'm really glad I have not remembered; that was something that should be forgotten. He has a new life with parents who love him.

There's no way he could remember us, he was six months old when he left us, but I'm grateful that we were able to give him the love he needed for a little while until there was someone to give him love for the rest of his life.

Give your children love. If you can afford to give them advantages then that's all right, just so long as you do not fall into the error of thinking it can be a substitute for love.

And if you cannot afford everything you would like to be able to give your children, don't worry. The most precious thing you can give them, the one thing they cannot do without, is your love and if you give them love you have given them far more than all the things in the world.

CHAPTER 26

The Escape of Sister Anthony

I never knew any religious sisters in my youth. I was twenty-eight years old when I became a Catholic and it was not until after that I came to know nuns as persons.

I'm not sure what I thought about sisters before that. I'd met them only as a reporter, who, covering a story sometimes talked to a nun who was a hospital administrator. Then I was impressed by a kind of crisp efficiency.

But I know what I thought about sisters after I came to know them as an adult. They are as different as any group of people but in one thing they are alike—in their caring.

I was and am still a man who loves sisters.

I think I learned most about sisters from Sister Anthony. She was in charge of the orphanage at Nazareth, N.C., where we had the editorial offices of the *North Carolina Catholic.*

Almost all her years as a sister she had been at the orphanage. With so many children in her care, she could not afford to have favorites among them or even show them a motherly affection.

She spoke with a heavy Irish brogue, softened by many years in North Carolina. She taught the children a kind of self-reliance.

A child would come in, crying because someone had pushed him and skinned his knee.

"Now hush your crying," she'd say with a kind of gentle roughness. "You'll get far worse knocks in life than this and you better be prepared for it."

But the brusqueness of her voice was shown as a lie by the tender way she'd treat the skinned knee.

She was ill for awhile and in the hospital. I went to see her. One of the boys, Billy, who had been brought to the orphanage as an infant, had been there longest and was about twelve, told me when he heard I was going to visit her to tell her to get well soon.

She was feeling better when I came to visit her. "It's a joy to be away from those children," she told me. "The first peace and quiet I've had for years."

I started to tell her what Billy had told me to say and she waved her hands at me, "Spare me that. I'm away and I don't want to be bothered with it."

Later there was a pause in our talking and she looked at me and said, "Billy asked about me, did he?" Then almost as if she was ashamed of being sentimental she spoke again, "Enough of that. I'm glad to be away."

She wanted above all else to escape from the orphanage, she said. When she was back, scolding the boys and girls, telling them they had better get prepared for the hard knocks of life, she'd stick her head into my office and say, "Pray for my intentions, Dale." But I would stop her. "I'm not praying for any intentions until I know what they are," I'd say. And she would laugh and say, "You know very well what they are." She didn't get any prayers out of me for those intentions, not that it would have mattered. God knew Sister Anthony belonged to Nazareth and that Sister Anthony really wanted to stay.

It was years later, long after I'd left, that the orders finally came that she had always said she wanted. She was at an age she needed to take it easy and so she was reassigned to the motherhouse of the Sisters of Mercy at Belmont.

They said that when the car came to take her to Belmont she said how happy she was to finally get away from the orphanage. She climbed alone into the back seat and as they drove off the grounds at dusk she didn't even look back.

She fell asleep on the way back and the two sisters in the front seat didn't want to disturb her. It was a drive of a hundred miles and when they arrived they spoke to Sister Anthony. But somewhere along the way Sister Anthony had died. She never did escape from her Nazareth.

I've known thousands of sisters and the more sisters I know the more my admiration for them grows. I miss the habits that some sisters have discarded. I get a little irritated sometimes when I see photographs of sisters in dress that seems to me extravagantly secular—I remember one of a sister in knee boots and mini-dress—and sometimes things I read that the so-called new nuns say exasperate me, too. But I discover that when I meet the so-called new nuns, talk with them, I find in them the same qualities of dedication and love that I've always found in sisters.

CHAPTER 27
The Death of Joe

On the day I'm writing this I received five letters from people who have recently lost in death someone they loved.

We almost all will experience this pain of loss in our lives. There's no easy way to handle it but sometimes in the sharing of experiences there may be hints of explanations.

The trauma of the death of someone you love is real. There is nothing to be gained by denying it. All of the pretty sentiment, saying the one you loved who is dead is only asleep or has simply gone ahead, doesn't meet the emotional need.

When someone we love dies we are devastated and the devastation is natural. Even when we believe in eternal life, have a confidence in Heaven, the death of one we love is shattering.

It can be handled because it must be handled. While we live we must live as fully, as usefully and as happily as we can and so the only way we can be true to those who have died is to continue our own lives.

I know that is easier said than done. I have seen good people totally immobilized by the death of one they loved, not just for days or weeks or months but for the rest of their lives. It is not the way it should be but it is the way that it is and we should be careful we do not make judgments on the failures of others to recover from the trauma of the death of someone they love.

My first experience with the intense pain of loss came when I was a young man. I found it almost impossible to handle. It was not the first death in our family; there had been the deaths of grandparents, uncles and aunts, but for the young the deaths of older people are expected and while there is sorrow there is no intensity in the experience.

It was the death of Joe that was too much for me. He was my only brother but he was not just my brother but my closest friend. We'd shared a room as we grew up, were friends then, but when we came into adulthood we were closer than ever before.

He was a most unusual young man, possessed of a kind of charisma that is rare. He was a man of conviction. He organized the first union in our town and, as president of the United Automobile Workers local, battled some stiff opposition.

We were different in many ways. There was a time in Sunday School when the class disintegrated into disorder. The teacher, abandoning any effort at discipline, allowed the boys to control the class, telling jokes, sometimes crude jokes.

It was too much for Joe. He was a year older than I and he stood up, motioned to me to follow him and walked out. The difference between us was that I came back a couple of weeks later, volunteered to teach a class of younger boys. Joe stayed away.

I was away from home and from my brother when I

began the studies that brought me into the Catholic Church. It was not surprising this disturbed most of my family; after all they had not been on the same pilgrimage to the Church and I had not expected they could share my experience.

But Joe, whose mind was always in closeness with mine, asked if I would help him understand. We talked and he said he wanted to know more. He had never been baptized and he said that while he could not yet share my faith with me, he did believe he should be baptized. He was baptized on a Sunday; a week later he was near death.

His appendix had ruptured. Today there are drugs that would probably have prevented the spread of infection, would have saved his life. They weren't available then.

He lived four days and in those days we talked— long talks about spiritual things. There was reason to believe he was moving towards recovery but surgery was needed. It was while he was on the operating table that his heart began to give out on him. He was dying when they brought him to his room. His wife, Alice, carrying their third child, was beside him. My parents and the rest of us were beside him. He took Alice's hand with one hand, our father's with the other.

He spoke gently and quietly. When we were boys together there was a little formula we had when there was something hard we were going to try. Joe looked up, smiled and said, "One for the money, two for the show, three to get ready and four to go." And he died.

I stayed when the others left and closed his unseeing eyes—and I was totally devastated by my brother's death. I can understand the grief that encompasses you entirely; I experienced it with the death of Joe.

In the way people support each other, we all of us tried to show courage. Alice was magnificent in her grief. Their children, five and three, couldn't quite understand but they were helped by their mother. Our parents stayed their grief until they were alone together.

I firmed my will and made the funeral arrangements. When returning after the burial, the funeral director's limousine ran out of gas and we had to walk the last few blocks home. We laughed together because Joe would have enjoyed that bizarre ending.

But deep within myself I felt only rebellion. Not Joe, Joe who had so much to live for, who loved his family and was loved by them, who had such a brilliant future, not Joe.

It was not that I didn't believe in an afterlife. I did completely. It was just that it didn't seem right; it made no sense; it just wasn't fair.

I went to confession to the old monsignor who had been so long the pastor in our hometown and I had come to know after I'd become a Catholic. "Forgive me, Father, for I have been guilty of despair," I said. "Oh, no, you haven't," he said to me and went on to explain that what I was experiencing was not despair of God's love and mercy but the natural sorrow that comes in bereavement.

But what I had tried to confess shows what intense pain was with me. It was something I just could not handle. It continued that way for a long time. Joe died at noon on a Friday and for a year or more I never came to a noon on Friday that I did not weep, did not feel again that pain of loss too great to contain.

I learned something by my experience that has served me well in times of grief.

First of all, it is simply not true that we ever really get over the pain of loss of those we love. To expect that we will is to expect what we may possibly never experience. What does happen is that we simply learn to live with the wounds we bear. Our sense of loss never really disappears, we simply learn to make it a part of what we are. There comes a time when it becomes such a familiar part of ourself that the pain is eased, that it comes to have a certain sweetness in our life.

Second, we must not expect that we will understand everything. We are finite, God is Infinite. A part of the confidence we must have in God must show itself in our acceptance of the fact that we cannot expect we will ever understand everything. Why Joe died as such a young man I do not understand, nor will I ever understand it this side of Heaven. The difference is that I no longer even ask the question.

Sometimes we find hints of explanations in ordinary things. I received such a hint the first time I took my little girl to the doctor for a shot. She looked in fear as the doctor came with the needle. Then she looked at me. Was I going to allow this man to harm her? I loved her, she knew that, but I was just standing to one side, not defending her as this stranger came to hurt her. She made a desperate plea to me with her eyes. Then something even worse happened. The doctor, seeing she was going to struggle, asked me to come and hold her still as he gave her the shot.

Now it was beyond all understanding for little Marianne. Not only did the father she trusted allow this to happen to her, he cooperated with the one who was hurting her.

When she received the shot and she began to cry she looked at me, disbelief in her eyes. Why? Why? And I saw in her anguished disbelief the same anguished lack of understanding I had once had of the working of Providence.

What I had done was out of my love for her, was for her own good. I knew the pain it brought to her and I knew there was no way I could explain it to her, make her understand. Some day she could understand but now she could not.

And in that hint of an explanation I understood how it is with us when what happens to us, with the apparent assent of God, is beyond our understanding. We can only love God and trust God, knowing there are things that happen that are beyond our comprehension.

The devastating sorrow at the loss of someone we love is real and we should not deny our grief. There is nothing in our grief that denies our belief in God. We have a right to weep for our loss is real.

But because we must continue to live, because we

must be true to ourselves and to one we loved who is
gone from earth, we must go on living, usefully, joyfully, but we must never expect the sense of loss will
ever disappear. We learn to live with it. It becomes
such a natural part of us that it is absorbed in our
living. And we must learn to know we simply will not
really know why some things happen, not in this
world, we won't.

CHAPTER 28

When Your Child Is Retarded

"Our family is shattered. We have been told our newly-born little girl is retarded. It is too much for us to bear. We were so happy when she was born but the knowledge that she will never be a normal child has turned happiness into sorrow."

One of the greatest traumas a family can face is the birth of a retarded child.

We're better in our society than we used to be. We no longer hide our retarded children. We no longer try to pretend they do not exist. Yet most people do not come into contact with the retarded, have little understanding of retardation, and when they learn their own child is retarded they are emotionally shocked and often completely distraught.

They have a right to be. We have dreams for our children, hopes for their achievements. When we learn our child can never fulfill the dreams, that there is no hope even for normal achievement, the disappointment is natural.

Yet there can be joy and happiness in having a retarded child. Most parents of the retarded have learned this. It is a bittersweet happiness—no need to sentimentalize the situation and pretend it is not.

When those who have just learned their child is retarded come to me, and hundreds have, I can understand their distress, I can share the sorrow they feel. Our son, Guy, is retarded.

Barbara and I had been married five years without having a child. We had prayed we would have children and we were sad because we had none. So we went to the Shrine of St. Anne de Beaupré, ascended the staircase there on our knees, praying we would be given a child. In one of those strange coincidences that have happened so often, later I bought one of those Tru-Vue slide sets of St. Anne de Beaupré and there was a picture of the staircase, taken as we were ascending it. We hadn't even known a photograph was taken.

When we prayed for a child we promised that child to God. He took us at our word.

Guy was already named before he was born. He was to be Guy Edward, named for Barbara's brother who was just 23 when he was killed in France at the breakthrough at Bastogne.

The diagnosis of Guy's retardation was made soon after his birth. They called it Hurler's Syndrome, a combination of congenital disabilities, club-feet, malformation of the heart, incomplete bone formation, brain injury.

Dr. Murphy didn't spare the truth. It was quite possible that Guy might always be bedridden, she said; his development might remain that of an infant. It was likely he would survive a few years at most.

I wish I could remember all the thoughts that rushed through my mind. I can't. I was in a daze. I had seen retarded children, as we all have, but I'd never known anyone who was retarded. I'd never even known, among friends, a family that had a retarded child.

I was the one to tell Barbara. She was still in the hospital; it had been a difficult birth. I told her. I didn't tell her everything the doctors had told me. It was more than I wanted her to have to bear, but I told her our son was retarded.

She was quiet for awhile. Then she spoke. "We asked for a child," she said. "We didn't ask for a perfect child."

We made that necessary leap more easily than most, I think. It is a leap all parents of retarded must make, the leap from all the expectations to the reality, a leap to the acceptance that the child that has been given is retarded but is our child, to care for and to love.

Not everything that is said to parents of retarded children is helpful. Well-intentioned people told us that God must love us very much to have chosen us to be the parents of a retarded child. When someone told St. Teresa of Avila that God gave his heaviest crosses to his best friends, she said, "No wonder He has so few friends." But those who say things like this mean well and there is truth in it, I suppose, for the crosses we are given are gifts in a sense.

But it seems to me the best way to adjust to this cross, as to all crosses, is simply to accept that this is the way that it is and to proceed from this reality, continuing to live as fully, as usefully and as happily as possible.

I've been around retarded children and parents of

retarded children often in the years since Guy was born—for two years I directed a community program for retarded. I've been able to observe the way people meet the problem.

One of the saddest responses is that of parents who do not want to admit their child is retarded. They keep going to specialists, hoping someone will tell them their child is normal. The sadness is not only in the stress they place upon themselves but in the lack of acceptance they give to their child as that child really is.

Even sadder is the case of parents who reject their child. I know of one family that placed their child in an institution immediately upon discovering him to be retarded, never visited the child, never discussed him. This is such an unnatural thing to do that it is difficult to believe those parents can ever find happiness.

The response that is most frequent—and not the right response—is one of over-protection. Looking back on our response to Guy, I believe we were sometimes guilty of this.

Why this happens I can understand because I know why it happened with us. You love your child. You are sorry your child is retarded. You want to make up to him all that he has lost by being retarded. So you do not insist that your retarded child be taught discipline as you would teach it to your normal children. His situation is special so you treat him specially.

Because your retarded child is not like other children, you over-protect him, try to keep him from the falls, the bumps, that other children experience.

But this, even though it is understandable, is wrong. You are aware that your child is different than other children, you realize your child will always lack what other children have, so by extra care, extra privilege you attempt to supply something to replace those defects.

But your retarded girl or boy is a person and has the right to realize the fullness of whatever potentiality he or she has as a person. The acceptance of your retarded child must be as the child is, not as you see your child as deprived of some faculties and possibilities other children have, *but as your child is.*

Those who are retarded can learn to do many things. There are training programs for the retarded in many communities that begin almost from infancy. In most states, public school systems are required by law to provide classes for the mentally retarded. We are learning that by proper training those who are retarded can achieve far more than had been thought possible in the past.

In the community program I directed we had a workshop in which young men and women who were retarded performed useful tasks. Industries in the community found there were tasks that could be turned over to the workshop. The local telephone company brought telephones to the workshop to have the men and women who worked there make modifications on them.

In a very real sense, we must come to a place where we treat retarded children as if they were normal. I do not mean we can escape realization that the retarded are limited. They are and we should not pretend they are not. But we must, as we do with normal children, seek to bring them to the fullness of their potential, seek insofar as possible, to give them a sense of self reliance.

I am well aware there are different degrees of retardation and what is possible with some who are retarded may not be possible with others. But all deserve the right to be brought to the fullness of whatever potential there is.

What we must not do is to feel pity for our retarded children and because of this over-protect them, pamper rather than train them.

Once I spoke about this before a group of parents of the retarded. Some of them had brought their children with them and after the meeting was over one young man, perhaps 13, a Downs Syndrome youth, came to me. "I'm certainly glad you said what you said," he told me. "My mother certainly needed to hear it."

His mother had not allowed him to go to a summer camp for the retarded. She was afraid he might be injured, she was afraid he would be homesick. She was standing there when he spoke to me and she listened and, although it must have been difficult for her, she agreed he could go to camp. It turned out not only to be a good experience for him but for her, too.

In accepting your retarded child you cannot fail to realize your child's limitations but you must not set the limitations yourself. We had been told Guy might never get out of bed, that he would live only a few years.

But Guy grew up to walk and run, to play. His malformed heart still threatens his life—the doctors decided there was no possibility of successful surgery to repair it—but he is now 28 years old.

Guy is a loving person. He laughs a lot and makes people happy to be around him. He is greatly limited but within his limitations he lives happily. He loves Mass and he receives Communion. Sometimes, I think, he understands the truth about the Eucharist even better than theologians.

I wish Guy were normal, of course I do. But he isn't. He is my son and I love him—love him not as the young man he might have been but as the son he is.

That's the secret, although it isn't really a secret; if we are given children we must love them as they are.

And there are many satisfactions, in a sense perhaps more special satisfactions than we have from our normal children because even small achievements have an importance.

The other day there was a letter from Sister Mark, the Ursuline who is a teacher at Good Shepherd Manor, where Guy is now. She wanted to share with me something that had happened.

Father John Hardon, the Jesuit theologian, was at Good Shepherd for a community chapter of the Brothers of the Good Shepherd. There had been Mass earlier in the morning and Guy had been there and received Communion. Later in the morning Father Hardon celebrated his Mass with a Brother to serve him. Guy went by the chapel, saw there was Mass, hurried in. When it came time for Communion, Guy started to go forward but Father had not intended to give Communion and didn't see Guy. Guy didn't like it and he told Sister Mark he had wanted to receive Jesus.

Then as Mass ended Guy stood and started singing his church song—Sister Mark thinks it is to the melody of the Gregorian "Adoro Te Devote" but I don't know; I just know he likes to sing a song he calls his Jesus song, and Sister Mark said Father Hardon stood at the altar until Guy finished his song—and I know Guy well enough to know it was a long, long song.

That's Guy, my son, and I love him. Sometimes when I see signs of the leadership he might have shown, the compassion he possesses, I have a twinge of sadness for the man he might have been but it doesn't stay with me even a second. I love him for who he is.

I said there are small achievements that can give you great satisfaction. I remember one of them.

One day I was busy writing and Guy wanted my attention. I kept at my work. He'd come to me to show me pictures he had drawn and I said they were nice and went on working.

He wrote G U Y, the only word he knows how to write, and I said that was good and went on working. He was away for a little while and then he came to me, smiling big. "Look, Daddy," he said and handed me another piece of paper. There he had written, in big but crooked letters, D A L E.

How he'd written it, I do not know. He had never

done it before, he has never done it since. But he did it that day. He held it up to me proudly.

"That's very good, Guy," I said. "Do you want me to play with you now?"

He grinned and I left my typewriter and so we sat down and drew airplanes and cows and trains and I thought there must not be many fathers who would gain a sense of joy in seeing a twenty-year-old son's writing of a name.

CHAPTER 29

When to Remember, When to Forget

Maybe the hardest thing Jesus told us we must do is love our enemies.

There are injustices in the world and people suffer those injustices. It isn't easy to forget those whose unjust actions have touched you personally.

Some time in your life someone is going to do you wrong. Sure as you live someone is going to do you an injustice. Count on it because it is going to happen.

I've run into it, so will you. I'm not going to recount any of the injustices I've known because that would be contrary to the advice I'm going to give concerning them.

I suppose the natural reaction when someone does you an injustice is to get even, hurt the one who hurt you. That's the reaction many people have but it is the surest way in this world to harm yourself.

If you suffer an injustice then forget it. That's not easy advice but that's the only advice worth giving.

First of all, you should be prepared for some injustices in your life because that's the way the world is. If you understand that some time in your life someone is going to do you wrong, then you'll not be surprised when it happens. That way you'll not take it so personally, understanding it as just one of the results of the human condition.

156

But the second thing you have to understand is that if someone does you an injustice it is the problem of the one who did the injustice. It may give you some difficulties but it isn't your problem. If you respond to it with thoughts of revenge then you make it your problem.

Writing this I realize I could be misunderstood. I'm talking about personal injustice, not an injustice that involves a principle. If the injustice involves other people then you must battle against it—but not for your own sake but for others.

Had I been a Black man I would have battled against Jim Crowing, I would not have allowed myself to be pushed to the back of the bus. One of the happiest moments of my life came one Sunday in a Catholic Church in the South when an usher tried to seat a Black man in the corner of the back seat at the Church.

The Black man spoke firmly. "No thank you, Brother," he said to the usher. "They may Jim Crow me in the buses, they may Jim Crow me in the theaters, they may Jim Crow me in the restaurants, but no one Jim Crows me in my Church."

Now that's not the kind of injustice I'm talking about. That kind of injustice you have to battle. But battling that kind of injustice isn't just for yourself, for your own pride, but for principles that can't be surrendered. That kind of battling of injustice not only helped all Black people, it helped that usher, too, and he was the one who needed help most of all.

Nor am I talking about any kind of social injustice.

To fail to battle against social injustice is to cooperate in evil and no one should do that.

What I'm talking about are injustices that affect only you, that come just because in this world you're going to run into some people who are not going to treat you right.

Those are the kind of injustices that for your own good you need to put out of your mind, the kind you don't dare allow to churn inside you, the kind that are someone else's problem that you shouldn't allow to become your own.

I've known people who suffered personal injustices and allowed them to affect all the rest of their lives. They come to treasure the injustices and before long they are using the injustices as an excuse for their own failures.

I said that telling you to forget is not easy advice. I'm not sure that's true. I've made a point of forgetting and I've found that I really do forget. I said I wasn't going to speak of any personal injustices I've known because that would be contrary to the advice I was going to give. But to make my point about how forgetting does become natural I am going to tell of an experience I have had.

Some years back, a fellow who was drunk, driving too fast, went through a traffic signal and crashed into a taxi that was carrying my mother home from her last minute Christmas shopping.

When the news came to me in a city far off, I caught a plane and got to my home town in time to talk to my mother. She was her usual forgiving self. She said she hoped the man wouldn't be punished but she did hope he wouldn't drive like that again.

My mother died of her injuries. The funeral was the day before Christmas and the saddest Christmas of all our lives came the next day as we looked at the packages our mother had wrapped and the messages she had written for each of us on the cards tied to the packages.

I felt anger, maybe even something close to hatred, for the man who had caused her death but I decided that I didn't want to have thoughts of anger and I put the man out of my mind. Although I had known his name, I discovered I couldn't remember it at all. I have almost total recall but his name was simply banished from my mind.

About eight years later I returned to my home town to edit the daily newspaper I'd started working on when I was a teenager. One day I was looking through the morgue for something else when I came on the file of stories about my mother. I opened it up and started reading it. The last clipping was about her death. I hesitated to read it but I thought I should. After all, I might run into this man whose name I'd forgotten. It would be good for me to know it. So I read the story, learned his name again, felt the old animosity rising up in me. I told myself it was important that I remember his name just so that if I met him in my work I'd know not to say anything to him that might burden him.

Then I put the file back, closed the drawer and discovered I had again forgotten the name. I had just looked at the news story. I had seen his name and literally seconds later I didn't remember it. I never looked at that file again, I never will again. The name of that man is forever banished from my mind.

I'm certain there's a psychological explanation for this. I know nothing about that. I just know I don't want to remember and I don't. If you gave me a list of ten names and told me his was among those on the list I wouldn't recognize it. It is simply totally banished from my mind. It is possible to forget injustices.

But there is something that I practice that I believe is connected with the forgetting of injustices. I regularly remember those who have done good for me.

I don't mean that I do this in a general way. I do it specifically. I take time to think back to all the people who have been kind to me. There were so many—thousands of people—and I consciously recall their names and the kindnesses they offered to me. I can remember them all. I start at my childhood, thinking of all the people who have helped me and the ways they helped me. I remember not just their names but their faces and the things they did for me.

It is not only a satisfying thing to do; it is a humbling thing to do as well, because when you do it you realize how much you owe to others, how much you have been helped in whatever you've been able to accomplish by other people.

They really belong together—remembering people who have done good to you and forgetting people who may have done you wrong.

CHAPTER 30

The Hardest Decision

We are called on to make hard decisions in life. One of the hardest of all concerns what has come to be known as death with dignity.

There are new problems we face because of the progress of science. Medical science is able to prolong life today beyond hope of recovery. We are forced to face the very real problem of whether to continue extraordinary means for prolonging life or to permit the natural progress of death.

This is not the same question that is raised by the advocates of euthanasia. They would propose that when an illness is terminal, death should be induced when the patient asks that it be done.

The question of whether or not extraordinary means should be used to prolong life is of an entirely different nature. It is in no way the same as euthanasia, for death is not imposed but allowed to happen. Pope Pius XII many years ago said that it was not necessary to continue extraordinary means for the prolongation of life, that there is virtue in allowing death with dignity.

We can reach very satisfactory answers to this question, assure ourselves that it is right that people should be allowed to die with dignity, that it can even be wrong to prolong life by extraordinary means when hope for recovery has passed.

But problems we don't have, that we can consider in theory, are a whole lot easier than problems we do

have. When the problem of the question of the prolonging of life by extraordinary means becomes our
own problem it is an almost unbearable burden.

It is not an occasional or an isolated problem either.
Because the extraordinary means for the prolongation
of life exist and are constantly being further refined,
there are many people who will one day be faced with
the problem when someone they love is near death.

When this day comes all the answers that were so
easy when you considered the question in theory
become difficult. When can you really know there is no
hope for recovery? Medical science can achieve such
marvelous things. People everyone think to be dying
do sometimes recover, even when the doctors say there
is no hope. But even if there is no hope that medical
science can bring recovery, whatever humanly possible
has been done, cannot God perform miracles? Is
giving up, accepting that one you love has passed hope
for recovery, not failing to trust that prayer may
achieve what man cannot achieve?

And what are extraordinary means? What science is
able to perform almost routinely is called extraordinary, but is it really? What is considered extraordinary
today may not be extraordinary tomorrow. If life is
continued is it not possible that in that time gained
there might be some discovery that will offer recovery?
Is it not possible that what we consider extraordinary
means for prolonging life might, through other discoveries, become the ordinary way to continue life for
the utilization of new discoveries that will restore
healthy life?

The answer to questions that you are not really facing comes easily. When the question becomes your own, when you must make the decision yourself, then it becomes unbearably hard. But one day the decision may be your own and then you will discover how difficult it is—what a terrible burden it is. I know because I faced the decision once myself.

I don't offer my experience or my decision as a guide for others. What I decided I had to do I did. I have not allowed myself any sense of regret. There would be no use in that, but it was my own decision and I would not say it would have to be a decision of others. But we are all of us helped by the experience of others and so I offer you mine.

My dad was at seventy-five a man who had almost never been ill. There had been accidents that had hospitalized him but he had never been in a hospital for illness. As a matter of fact, I do not remember even a day that he had been ill in all his life.

When my mother died of injuries in an automobile accident, he was inconsolable. They had been close in a way that only a few husbands and wives are close. In all my life I never knew either of them to say an angry word to the other. They shared everything, liked nothing more than being together.

When Mother died it was as if a part of Dad had died, too. He would sit at home, beside the chair where once she had sat, and weep quietly.

He told me how it was. "It was hard when Joe died," he said, speaking of my brother who had died as a young man, "but then I had Mom. We could put our arms around each other and weep together. It was hard but we could bear it together. But now without Mom, it's too much for me."

Then, fearing that he might have hurt me and being a man who would never have knowingly hurt anyone, he said, "I have you and Margaret and Betty. But, Dale, it's different. Mom and I were one person."

I've read reports that say under emotional distress sometimes cancer develops. Maybe that was the explanation. Maybe the cancer had been developing all along, I don't know, but six months after my mother's death my father was found to have cancer.

He told me it had surprised him. "I've always been well. I'm not used to being sick. But most of all I didn't think it would turn out to be cancer. I always thought that if I had cancer I would know it, feel it inside of me."

When they operated the doctor thought he had caught it. Dad was a strong man and he battled against his illness. His grief was inconsolable, he had lost the most important reason for living, but Dad was simply by nature not a man who would give up and allow himself to die.

It didn't take him long to recover from the surgery. He regimented his body, forced back his strength, and being a man who was incapable of not working was back at work, spending evenings working in the garden where he grew the finest vegetables and the most beautiful flowers in the neighborhood.

He was working when it happened. There was internal hemorrhaging, he passed out and was rushed to the hospital. There they discovered the cancer had spread. There was nothing they could do; his illness was terminal.

He battled it for two months, enduring pain so intense that his face would turn white, but without a word of complaint. He talked with us of many things, thought about eternal things. The cancer that was ravaging his body didn't find it easy to conquer him. But more and more his body had to depend on what he called "contraptions," for sustenance, for elimination.

He didn't like it. He was a man. They were reducing him to those contraptions. He'd been a man from the time his father died, when Dad was just a boy. He had gone to work when he was twelve and he had worked all his life.

Most of his life he was a Western Union lineman and the outdoor life, the walking along the lines, the climbing of poles and the repair of wires broken by storm or ice, had kept him strong. Although he had almost no formal education, he had educated himself. He was a man respected by other men, respected by the people in the community. The first time I remembered having pride in my father came when I was a first grader and walking home with other boys. I heard an older boy ahead of us say, "You better cut out the cussing when you go by the Francis house. Mr. Francis doesn't allow it."

There were other things he didn't allow. He didn't allow anyone to use epithets for other people. We were the only kids in school who said "catch a fellow by the toe." Around Dad you didn't use other words for people. "He is an Italian," my dad said once, correcting a man who had referred to another man with an ethnic epithet.

And around Dad you didn't say anything bad about anyone. "If you can't say something good about a person then don't say anything at all," he would say if we passed on some scandal we had heard.

In the town where we lived in my earliest years, he was the head of the school board, a man of substance in the town, and probably the only man in town (except for the two Catholics who lived there and had crosses burned on their front lawns) who was not a member of the Ku Klux Klan.

Once we had gone to a funeral and the Klan marched in and my dad was the only man there without the hood and robe. When afterwards a man who must have been a friend of his came up to him to speak, Dad said, "Talk to me later, John, when you are not afraid to show your face."

For all his firmness he was a man who did not show anger. There was no harshness in him. Before he and mom was married—he waited until he was thirty-four when he met mom who was twenty-one—he was the foreman of a road gang of linemen who travelled around the country, raising new lines, going where floods or storms had torn down lines. The men who had worked with him through those years remained his friends through all his life and they'd come to visit. More than one told a story about him that they must have passed around for years.

Another lineman was working at the top of a pole

and Dad was working below. The man on the pole dropped his pliers and they shot down and caught Dad on the shoulder. Dad looked up, they said, and very quietly said, "Now if I was a cussing man I'd say doggone."

That was the man who was dying before us. He was battling it and it wasn't doing any good. We were alone one afternoon in the hospital room.

"There's something I want you to do for me, Dale," he said.

There wasn't anything in this world I wouldn't do for my father and I said, "Of course, Dad, whatever you want." I think I thought he was going to ask me to get a cold wash cloth, something like that.

But he said, "I want you to ask Doc Hogle to take all these contraptions away and let me die."

It stunned me. I knew he wasn't going to get well. I'd gone over it with the doctors and they said there wasn't a chance. But I had hoped there would be months, at least weeks. I wanted to talk with him all I could. I knew he was going to die but I didn't want him to die. Now he was asking me this.

"But, Dad," I said. "You've got to hold on, maybe you'll get well again."

He looked at me with exasperation in his face. "Now, Dale," he said, "you know that isn't true. We don't lie to each other. I'm not going to get well. You know that and I know that. I don't want to die with all these contraptions hooked up to me. Do what I ask you to do, Dale."

I didn't promise I would, I didn't say I wouldn't. I

didn't know what I should do. The problem in the abstract I would have been able to solve easily, the problem when it was my own was almost more than I could handle.

We talked about other things. I had to change the subject but my mind was filled with what he had asked me to do. Just before I left he reached out his hand to me. "Please, Dale," he said.

So I did what he asked me to do. Doc Hogle thought about it. "It's what he wants?" he asked me. "It's what he wants," I answered. "What about you?" I shook my head. "I don't know. It's what he wants; it's what he asked me to do."

The next day they took away all the contraptions. He thanked me. "I'm sorry I had to ask you, Dale," he said, "but it was the right thing to do."

Two days later he died, conscious until his last moments, a man unencumbered by contraptions, a man who stood erect even while he lay dying in a hospital bed.

Did I do the right thing? Did I make the right decision? I never even ask myself those questions. I did what I decided I should do. There would be no use in going back over the decision. But what I can say is that it was hard. It was maybe the hardest thing I ever had to do in my life.

Other people will be facing the same decision. The way medical science has developed means for the prolongation of the signs of life, more and more people will be facing that awe-ful decision.

You'll find discussions of it again and again in the newspapers and the magazines. There will be facile answers that will tell you what to do. If you are wise you'll think about it now, find the truths before you are called upon to act on them.

But I can promise you that if the day comes you are the one who must make the decision all the easy answers will crumble, all the questions will rise shouting in your mind, and it will be a hard decision, the hardest you'll ever have to make.

CHAPTER 31
Life Is Terminal

There are often letters from people who have learned they, or those close to them, are terminally ill.

Sometimes they can have hope that what was once a terminal illness may now be treated successfully—that is true today of Hodgkin's Disease, which once we came to know as the enemy.

It seems strange to think that once the words Hodgkin's Disease were unfamiliar to me.

We had known something was wrong. It was in May when Barbara first started coughing. Because I've always believed that if you have a medical problem you should get to a doctor and get it checked, we went to the doctor the very first week.

He diagnosed it as a bronchitis. Later when it persisted and tests showed nothing, he sent her to an allergist. Barbara had always had a sensitivity to pollens and so he treated her. It seemed to help.

The illness was never disabling. Neither of us really thought of it as an illness at all, just a bothersome allergy. During the whole time she was under doctor's care, she had all the tests that she could have been expected to have.

We really knew something had to be seriously wrong because of a photograph. We were asked to be the godparents for a baby boy born in the parish. There were photographs taken and one of them was given to us.

When you are with someone all of the time you are unaware of physical changes. But when Barbara saw the photograph she was surprised. There were lines in her face she had not had before, there was a kind of grayness in her complexion. "I look like someone who is very seriously ill," she said. And, although I had not really been aware of it before, I could look at the photograph and see that it was true.

She had started having a low-grade temperature but the allergy specialist said this was not inconsistent with the effects of allergies. He was not really greatly concerned. That reflected no incompetence on his part. He had treated her for allergies since she was a little girl. He had seen patterns in her reactions to allergies not really much different than those she had now. He had x-rays taken when the coughing persisted but there was no indication of any problem.

We had little money but I decided in mid-winter that it might help if she had some sunshine. The way things always seemed to happen for us, it turned out to be possible. There was a letter in the mail from an old friend, an Episcopalian priest, Father Clarence Petrie. There were things he wanted to talk about. He wondered if we would come to Clewiston, Fla., to visit for awhile. He had arranged for us to have an apartment for three weeks; it would cost only fourteen dollars a week. We could afford that and so we went.

The sunshine helped. The cough subsided. Being with Mr. Petrie, who had spiritual problems he wanted to talk about, turned us both from thinking about her illness to thinking about Mr. Petrie. She seemed better

but the last week the fever came back, now 102 degrees
and more. A doctor there said he could not find the
cause; he urged us to get to the hospital for a thorough
checkup when we returned home.

On the day we returned to the North Carolina city
where we lived there was one of the portable x-ray
buses parked downtown, urging people to step in for
an x-ray of their chest. Barbara had an x-ray taken;
they said they would mail her the results.

Dr. Charlie Norris, who had been Barbara's classmate in grade school at St. Patrick's, was our family
doctor and he agreed that a good thorough check at
the hospital was necessary.

He wasn't worried, Barbara wasn't worried, but I
had a feeling of fear, the kind that goes through your
whole body and leaves you with cold sweat.

It was like a visit for Barbara at Mercy Hospital.
The sisters were old friends. She was given a room but
she didn't stay in bed. She visited with the sisters, with
friends who were in the hospital, went for her tests but
not with any sense of being a patient.

I literally sweated out the results of those tests. The
worry grew for me. The next day I went to the
sister who was in charge of the hospital and told her
how worried I was.

She smiled. "There's really nothing to worry
about," she said. "Barbara is all right. It is a good
thing to get everything checked but I'm sure she's all
right. We visited yesterday and she surely doesn't seem
ill."

To assure me she called the laboratory. "Can you

give me the report on the tests on Barbara Francis?" she asked someone. The smile vanished from her face, her voice lowered, "I see," she said, "I see."

She put the phone down; for a few seconds she sat there, looking down at her desk. Then she turned to me. "I'm sorry, Dale. It really is very serious. Charlie wants to talk with you."

He was on the first floor in the room they had for doctors. There was pain in his face.

"It's Hodgkin's Disease," he said without any preliminaries. Hodgkin's Disease? I'd never even heard of it. That name that was to become so familiar, that disease that was to become such an old enemy that it seemed almost like an old friend, was something I'd never even heard of before.

"But what is Hodgkin's Disease?" I asked.

"It is a cancer of the lymph glands. I'm sorry, Dale, but it is terminal."

Terminal? Even that word was unfamiliar. I knew it but not as something that had any meaning in my own life. Charlie went on talking, telling me more of the illness, saying there could be no specific prognosis, that it might be months, that it could be years. There was really no way of really knowing, except at this time there was no hope for recovery. The illness was terminal. Terminal. That word kept ringing in my head, almost bursting the inside of it.

"Have you told Barbara?" I asked him.

"No," he said. "I thought you would want to do that. Sometimes it is best not to tell patients everything. I thought you should be the one to decide."

It was right that I should be the one to make the decision. If she was told, I was the one who had to tell her. I knew Barbara and there really wasn't any decision that had to be made.

"She will want to know," I said.

Charlie nodded his head, "Yes, I think she would want to know."

"I'll tell her," I said.

I can hide nothing; everything goes to my face. When I walked into her room she knew something was wrong by my look.

"You look like the bearer of sad tidings," she said smiling.

So I told her. How I told her I do not know, but I told her.

The smile didn't leave her face. "I thought it was going to be serious," she said. "This Hodgkin's Disease, what's that?"

So I explained. I told her there were large growths around her lungs, that the snip from a swelling in her armpit had given them the diagnosis.

"It is terminal," I said.

She laughed, "Life is terminal."

She comforted me when I had come to comfort her. "Look," she said. "We'll fight this old Hodgkin's Disease. We won't give up. There's lot of life in this old girl yet, you just wait and see."

And then she talked of the children, Guy and Marianne. "They are too young to understand. If I have to be in the hospital we'll just say mother isn't feeling well."

She was still smiling when I left. I drove home in a daze. Fannie Carr was taking care of the children and she would be waiting to get home. No one had taken in the mail so I took it out of the box. There was a magazine, two or three bills and a card from the Mecklenburg County Tuberculosis Association addressed to Barbara.

"Congratulations," was the cheery greeting. "Your x-ray shows you are in good health. Be sure to have regular checkups."

Marianne was not yet three. She came running to me. "How's Mommy?" she asked. "She said I should tell you and Guy that she loves you very much and she sends you each a kiss," I said and I hugged her hard, holding her tight.

I didn't allow myself tears but I wept inside.

Fannie was concerned. She had worked for Barbara's parents for many years and had known Barbara from childhood. "How is Miss Barbara?" she asked me when we were alone. "She's really pretty sick," I said, "but I think she is going to be all right." "Thank the Lord for that," Fannie said.

I gave the children their supper, said their prayers with them and put them to bed. I sat in the living room, a thousands thoughts rushed through my mind. Barbara was just thirty-eight; Barbara was going to live to be a hundred. The phone rang.

It was one of the student nurses; I'd known her from the time she was a little girl.

"Dale," she started out, children somehow always called me by my first name. "There's something I want to know. We've been talking about it. Does Barbara know what her illness is?"

"Yes, she knows," I said.

"I knew it," she said. "The other girls said it couldn't be true. She was out in the hall, talking and laughing with the nurses. She went down to Mrs. Beatty's room and was cheering her up. They said she couldn't know, that no one who knew could be laughing and talking. But I knew, Dale, because I know Barbara."

I sat down and tears came. Yes, she knew Barbara.

I need to know things; whenever there is something new in life I study it, try to know it as well as I can. So I ordered all the books that were available on Hodgkin's Disease, medical books that Charlie got for me. I studied them carefully, read every word. What I read didn't give me hope but I got to know our enemy, know it so well that there was nothing that was known about it that I didn't know.

Barbara still didn't allow herself to be a patient. She was home a few days later. They began x-ray treatment, bombarding the areas where there were tumors. Charlie had warned the x-rays might make her nauseated but almost by an act of will she didn't allow that to happen.

She started working again at the Catholic Information Center we had in downtown Charlotte. It was almost as if there was no illness at all.

She took it all so casually that it bothered me. She

did everything just as she had done before. She didn't rest, she didn't even seem to be doing anything to take care of herself.

So one Sunday afternoon I talked to her. "Look," I said, "you've got to take this seriously. You've got to take it easy; rest so you'll keep your strength. Don't you understand you have a terminal illness?"

"All right, all right," she said. "I hereby promise I will take my terminal illness seriously."

Then she started laughing and I started laughing and we couldn't stop laughing. The doorbell rang. We opened the door. It was Art Linsky and his new wife. We'd known Art at Notre Dame and he had come to live in Charlotte, too.

"What's so funny," he said.

"Just a private joke," I said and we laughed some more. When they had left we laughed again.

"Why didn't you tell them what we are laughing about?" she asked me.

"How are you going to explain you're laughing because your wife won't take her terminal illness seriously," I said. We laughed some more and Marianne came in. "What you are laughing about?" she asked.

"Just a private joke," Barbara said and we laughed some more.

We had two dreams, far off dreams because there was no early chance of their realization. We wanted one day to visit Europe, to go to Lourdes, to visit

Rome, to visit Fatima in Portugal and to go to Spain
and France and England. The other dream was that
one day we'd live for a year or two in another country.

Now there was no time for dreams in some far off
future, there weren't years ahead of us, there were only
months. But I told her I had made a decision.

"We're going to make that trip to Europe," I said.

"Why not the moon as a side trip?" she asked.
"You do understand we have no money, don't you?"

I understood. I'd left a good position at the University of Notre Dame to come to the least Catholic city in
the entire nation to open a Catholic Information
Center in the heart of the city.

By every sensible reckoning it was a foolhardy
venture. It wasn't even what I had planned to do. I
wanted a Catholic Information Center, all right, and I
had decided I would try one. But I wanted to start it in
a city where there was some possibility of supporting it
by sales of books and religious articles.

I had been in correspondence with Monsignor Barry
at St. Patrick's on Miami Beach. He liked the idea,
said there was need for such a center, was certain that
it could be self-supporting and that there would be
financing to get it started.

Then Bishop Vincent Waters, who was the man who
had started me in service of the Church years before
when we began the *North Carolina Catholic* together,
visited Notre Dame and I told him of my plans.

"Why would you want to go to Florida?" he asked
me. "We need a Catholic Information Center in North

Carolina. Forget about Florida and come back home to North Carolina. You have tar on your heels, you're not going to get it off. You come to North Carolina."

I tried to explain that it just wasn't good business sense, that the center had to be self-supporting. But he laughed, "Don't worry about that. It is the center that is important. Come to North Carolina."

A few days later he wrote a letter. He would provide $25,000 if we would come for four years. If there were profits then I could pay him back. The money would be delivered in installments, enough at the beginning to get the stock.

So we went to Charlotte, N.C. The center opened on Tryon Street, next door to the biggest Baptist Church in the city. It was the most successful financial disaster I've ever known. When some over-enthusiastic Southern Baptists soaped our windows with some anti-Catholic epithets the pastor of the Baptist church came over to apologize and to welcome us. The rector of the Episcopal church across the street became a regular visitor. In four years more than 250 clergymen of other churches in the Piedmont area of North Carolina stopped by to visit us.

True to my own lack of business common sense, we established some rules for what we had to sell. "We'll have nothing that glows in the dark or whose eyes follow you wherever you go," I decided concerning the religious articles. We bought the finest statues; there was a good selection of Beuron art. There were statues from Grailville. The Sacred Heart statues were subdued; I'd found a supplier from France. Our prints came from New York Graphic.

The some 4,000 books were carefully selected. A professor from Princeton University, passing through the city, stopped by and said it was the finest selection of Catholic books he had ever seen. "But how can you sell books like these in the South?" he asked me.

The answer to that was we couldn't, not many at least. There were readers. It may be that we sold more of the works of St. John of the Cross and St. Teresa of Avila than any other Catholic store in the country but you don't get rich on sales like that.

While we did sell many of the finest religious articles we stocked I had kept the markup low; getting things into homes I thought was more important than making a profit.

It was successful. It first of all gave Catholics a sense of pride because people in the city talked with favor about the center we called The Sign of the Cross. That was important in a city where Catholics felt themselves to be a beleagured minority.

And there were many converts. We didn't give instructions in the center but I talked with people when they came by with questions and arranged for instructions with priests in the area, choosing the priests carefully according to what I thought to be the needs of the people I sent to them. There were more than 200 people who started their instructions from the Sign of the Cross. Many were young people; one was a student at Davidson, the Presbyterian college some 20 miles away. He became a Catholic, then a priest and years later he was assistant pastor at a parish to which I belonged.

Through the center I started a radio program at WBT, the city's most powerful radio station. I answered questions about the Church that people telephoned in and it reached people from New England to the Bahamas. *Newsweek* wrote about it, carried my picture at the telephone.

Most of all, it was successful in the way it created a friendship among people who were not Catholics and had no intention of ever becoming Catholics. Ministers were friendly to us. A Lutheran pastor regularly urged people to visit us and even set up a display of articles in the vestibule of his church one Sunday.

It was successful all right but not financially. Barbara was right when she said it was foolish to think of making a trip to Europe. We had no money, we barely had enough to put food on our table, to run our old car, to meet the house payments.

But I didn't care. If we were going to make our trip to Europe, we had to make it now. We had no guarantee of a tomorrow.

I went down to the Carolina Motor Club. I got all the books, started planning our trip. We would go first to Fatima, then to Spain where we had friends in the Opus Dei, then to Rome and Assisi and Florence and Venice. From there we would go to Paris, to visit Notre Dame and 23 Rue de Bac and finally to London.

I came home with the itinerary all worked out and

told Barbara where all we would go. Barbara laughed, "It's a wonderful trip. I'll be glad to go with you." She laughed, "Now let's look at the old bank account."

He phoned on a Sunday morning, soon after we'd come back from Mass.

His name, he said, was George Strake. He was from Houston. He knew me from the column I wrote in *Our Sunday Visitor*. He said he would like to talk to me about something. He didn't have a car and wondered if we could come to the airport to see him.

He took us aboard his private plane to talk to us. It was fixed up like a living room. The children climbed over the furniture as we talked.

He explained he had heard of Barbara's illness. I do not remember if he told us how. He said he thought we should go to Europe, to Fatima, to Lourdes, to Rome, to Assisi, to Florence, to Venice, to Paris and to London. He had arranged it all. He had the tickets, he would provide us with other money for incidentals. He wanted it to be his gift to us.

We had told no one of what we had planned. I hadn't even prayed about it. Praying for things for ourselves is something that just never occurs to me. But I had planned the trip we would take and in every detail it was the same as the one George Strake had planned for us.

We thanked him. We were very grateful but probably we were not as surprised as he would have expected us to be. He was a good man, a man I'll never forget, but somehow I must have expected him.

When we got back home Barbara picked up the folders, looked them over. Then with her Southern accent she said, "Now don't that beat all."

There were many things that were happening at the same time, some good, some not so good.

I wasn't well organized and Barbara wasn't much better. In all of the stress of learning of Barbara's illness, I'd not taken care of bills. Our hospitalization insurance had come due. The period of grace for paying it passed before I even opened the envelope. We had lost our hospitalization just at the time we needed it most. That wasn't good.

But years before I had talked with Bishop John Noll, the founder of *Our Sunday Visitor,* about a plan I had for a national Catholic information bureau. He had provided for the bureau in Washington and he wrote me now. He wanted me to be its director, no need for me to move to Washington, he said. I could commute. There was a sizeable check with the letter; he thought we might need some money to meet hospital expenses. We did.

But perhaps most important of all there was a letter from our old friend, Lucile Hasley, a beautiful writer, a beautiful person. She said I was foolish not to ask the prayers of the friends among the readers at *Our Sunday Visitor.* I was writing an entertainment column, reviewing movies and television programs. There didn't seem any way to work something like that into the kind of a column I was writing but I talked with Bill Fink at OSV about it and he said I should do

it. So I wrote about Barbara and asked the prayers of
the readers. There were literally thousands of letters
and the prayers we received must have been in the
millions and the most wonderful readers in this world
ceased being just readers and became our friends.

The trip to Europe was all that we dreamed it would
be. There was almost no one at Fatima when we were
there but the bareness of it all seemed just right. A
young couple were being married at a little chapel in
the great courtyard in front of the huge church and we
knelt with their friends and prayed for their happiness
and cheered them as they walked out of the chapel.

Friends from Opus Dei met us in Madrid. Mon-
signor Escriva, the founder of Opus Dei, had asked
that we should be taken to the grave of Isidoro
Zorzano, a member of Opus Dei who had died of
Hodgkin's Disease and who is now nearing beatifica-
tion. Isidoro was buried in the tomb with Monsignor
Escriva's mother and father. Our friend, Father
Joseph Musquiz, then, as now again, head of the Opus
Dei in the United States, had arranged that members
of the Opus Dei should be our guides.

We went from there by train to Lourdes, which we
decided was the most beautiful place in the world. The
Bishop of Lourdes greeted us, talked with us about
many things and gave us a piece of rock from the
grotto as a souvenir.

Mr. Strake had provided for us in Rome. Some
years before he had met Msgr. Giovanni Montini and
told him in passing that if there was ever some special

need the monsignor should call on him. A few weeks later Monsignor Montini called on him. The Vatican wanted to begin excavations under St. Peter's in the hope they might find the tomb of St. Peter. It would cost about a million dollars. George Strake, whose charities were so great that no one really knows of them all, sent the money for the excavations. It was done, as were most of the things Mr. Strake did, without any publicity.

When Mr. Strake told them friends of his were coming to Rome, there was nothing they wouldn't do for us. Msgr. Joseph McGeough, an American in the papal diplomatic corps, was our host.

He took us in his car to all the places we wanted to visit—to Netunno and the chapel of St. Maria Goretti, to the room where my favorite saint, St. Benedict Joseph Labre had died. Monsignor Montini, who was to become Pope Paul, welcomed us. We talked a long time of the plans I had for the information bureau in Washington and he was enthusiastic. Pope Pius XII was not well. He was having no audiences, but he came to his window to give the crowd in St. Peter's Square his blessing.

We visited Assisi and Florence and Venice. We were in the cathedral in Venice when Cardinal Roncalli came into the Church alone. He moved from the altar to a place not far from us and we introduced ourselves and talked with him a little while, never even guessing that this heavy old man would be the next Pope.

We were in Milan for only a few hours but we

received a strange blessing. The first church we entered was just starting Benediction, a devotion we loved. When Benediction was over we walked to another church. As we entered, Benediction was just beginning. By most remarkable coincidence we visited five churches that afternoon and each time just as Benediction began.

"I don't remember having been Benedicted so many times in all my life," Barbara said.

Paris was wonderful because the chapel at 23 Rue de Bac drew us most of all. We were four days in Paris. We never saw the Louvre, we missed all the places tourists always go. We visited the great white Church of Sacre Coeur but only for a little while. Almost all of our time was spent in the chapel where the incorrupted body of St. Catherine Laboure lies, the holy woman who was given the Miraculous Medal, and where the tomb of St. Vincent de Paul is. It drew us again and again and we spent most of the four days kneeling there.

London gave us lots of book stores, Mass at the Farm Street Church celebrated by Father Martin D'Arcy—a priest we had long admired for his writings.

We stayed at the Claridge's—Mr. Strake had arranged everything first class. The last evening we had dinner in the dining room where an orchestra was playing and people were dancing on a ballroom floor.

I'd never learned to dance. Barbara was a good dancer and liked to dance, but after a few hopeless efforts to teach me she had given up.

The orchestra was playing, I forget the song, I should remember things like that but I don't.

"Hey, double left foot, how about one last dance," she said.

So we got up and we danced our last dance.

We were given seven years. When death came it was almost seven years to the day since Barbara had first become ill.

They were seven busy years. One of our dreams for the future already realized, we decided the other should come true, too. We were going to live for awhile in a foreign country.

It was with the help of friends of Opus Dei that we started making our arrangements. The secretary for Bishop Angel Hererra of Malaga, Spain, was a member of the Opus Dei. Bishop Hererra had been a prominent newspaperman before he entered the priesthood. His secretary had talked with him about us and he wanted us to come to live and work in his diocese.

They sent us photographs of available housing. We started making our plans. But one thing I learned a long time before, plans I made had a way of being changed without anyone really consulting me. I was enrolled to start classes at Yale when it turned out I was going to Notre Dame instead. I was opening a center in Miami Beach and I wound up in Charlotte, N.C.

And that was the way it happened about our plans for Malaga. My mother died. My father was ill; Barbara's father was ill. Going so far away didn't seem right.

Then there came a letter from Bishop Alberto

Martin y Villaverde of Matanzas, Cuba. I'd written a column about the need for parish team ministry, an idea that then had not been discussed at all. He said he wanted to try what I had proposed and he thought it would be good if I came to live in his diocese for awhile. He said he could offer nothing in remuneration, that his diocese was desperately poor, but that he had felt he should write to me.

He knew nothing of our plans to live in another country. We had many years before asked the guidance of the Holy Spirit in all that we did. It seemed to us that this was the Holy Spirit calling. Laymen in the town took over the operation of The Sign of the Cross. The four years had passed but the financial situation was almost hopeless. I gave up my position in Washington; a new bishop moderator for the work was a good man but so cautious there was nothing I could really do.

Bill Fink at *Our Sunday Visitor* sent a check for $500 to meet the expense of getting to Cuba. We sold our house. It was in a day in which real estate wasn't appreciating and we got out of it only enough to pay off the mortgage—nothing of our equity remained.

I had a total income of about $300 a month. We had almost no savings. We packed the old Ford with all our worldly possessions and I drove to Miami, took it aboard an overnight ferry to Havana. Barbara, Marianne and Guy flew to Havana and we met there.

Bishop Alberto met us in Matanzas. He had a hotel for us but he had not found us a place to live. He said he hoped we would choose our own place, anywhere in the diocese.

We drove east from Matanzas the next day, going through some villages. At Coliseo we turned to the south and drove down a road lined with palm trees. There was a hill and when we came to the top of it we stopped to look down on a little village. Just back of a white towered church there was a great hill and on top of it there was a little chapel.

"That's where we are going to live," I said. We stayed awhile looking at the town that would be our home. "I wonder what the its name is?" I said.

It was San Miguel de los Banos.

We drove into the town and saw a priest walking along the street. He spoke almost no English. We spoke less Spanish, but the idea of what we wanted was understood. Less than an hour later we had rented a furnished home—for $100 a month—and we stayed that night in our new home. It was in the country, outside the little town, and there were *bohios* around it, palm-thatched homes, many of them with dirt floors.

And the people of the *bohios* became our best friends. Through readers of *Our Sunday Visitor* we were able to open a school. What we had not known was that there was another home in the village, the summer home of Cardinal Artega. We became friends with him. We met other people. I started writing a column for the *Havana Post*. I came to know people in important places. Readers of *Our Sunday Visitor* came to visit us. Bishop Martin appointed me as director of Defense of the Faith in his diocese.

The story of the days in Cuba would make a book but there is no room to tell of it all here. Most of all we made friends. Some years later I returned to Cuba and a taxi driver took me about Havana and finally to San Miguel. In Havana we had visited many people in high places, people the driver knew by reputation. In San Miguel the friends I visited lived in *bohios*. A little black boy, whose grandmother conducted voodoo services in the valley and was a woman I visited often, saw me half a block away and started shouting, "Mi Americano, Mi Americano" and several feet away in his run toward me leaped into the air to grab me around the neck and hold on to me. A little girl whose brothers and sisters always had Sunday dinner with us came running to me and kissed me again and again.

The taxi driver shook his head as we drove from San Miguel. "I've never seen anyone who knew such different people," he said. There was the joy of living in Cuba and that was the sadness of it, too. One beautiful day, Barbara had said it. She looked at the beautiful green hills, the tall palm trees. "What a paradise this would be if only the people didn't have to suffer so much."

It became necessary for us to leave. After nearly two years of relative remission the fever had returned. A doctor treated Barbara in Havana but although he was a good doctor, we thought we should be back in the States.

Marianne had come to school age. She had gone to kindergarten at a little public school in San Miguel but now she spoke Spanish almost entirely. We wanted her educated in English.

We started making our plans to return to the United

States. I had said in my column that we would return and that we were trying to decide where to go. There were a wide variety of opportunities. A woman in California said she would give us her beach home if we would come live there. There were offers from pastors, from schools. We finally decided we would go one of three places—it would be Miami, El Paso or San Diego. That much we knew for certain but which of the three it would be we didn't know.

And then it happened again. There would be a stack of letters in the muddle that was my desk and I'd pick them up and the letter on the top would always be one from someone in Austin, Texas. It happened not once but several times.

I told Barbara about it. "Do you suppose that means something?" I asked. She said we should wait and see. But Austin wasn't in our plans at all and I resented a little that letters from Austin kept appearing. They were just from people saying we should come there. None of them were letters offering anything for me to do. "It's going to be El Paso or Miami or San Diego," I said firmly, a little irritated that the idea of Austin had intruded.

Then a letter from the president of St. Edward's University came. He wanted me to come to the university. I would come as his assistant, as an idea man. My title would be director of public relations but what he had in mind was something much more than this.

So I gave up. "I guess it's supposed to be Austin," I said. So I wrote that I would come in the late summer. It was spring, and he wrote back to say he was pleased.

When we arrived the whole situation had been changed. There had been a split of provinces. The president of the university had been placed in the eastern province. A new young president had been chosen. I don't know that he had ever even heard my name. All he knew was they had a new director of public relations. The job I had thought I was coming to simply didn't exist. I wound up writing press releases for hometown papers about new students at the university.

Because they had to justify my salary, although it was not large, I taught some classes. But that was not why I'd come to Austin, that's not why the Holy Spirit had been so persistent. It wound up I was supposed to start a diocesan paper and I did.

Bishop Louis Reicher was a plain-spoken man. He wanted a diocesan paper. He didn't want to start it himself. He wanted me to start it. That was fine with me except it turned out when he said that he meant it exactly the way he said it. He would make it his official paper but it had to be my paper. I had to start it with my own money. My own money? I didn't have any money.

But I started it. A friend from my youth, Jim Houser, came out from Ohio to handle the business end. *Our Sunday Visitor* gave me a boost, let me start an "Operation Understanding" edition for clergymen of other faiths along with it which gave it an extra circulation base. We started it. It paid for itself, not much more than that, but it paid for itself. It had a good circulation throughout the diocese. When I left Austin I gave it to the diocese. They took it over, paid some $2,000 in outstanding bills, and that was all it ever cost the diocese during the three-and-a-half years.

There was a cemetery back of St. Edward's, a beautiful place alongside a busy highway. "I suppose that is where I'll be buried," Barbara said, the day we arrived in Austin, looking at it not with sadness but interest. It was.

We lived in Austin from 1957 until Barbara died in 1961. It was a difficult but productive time for Barbara. She wrote a column for our paper; kept working on the novel Doubleday had sent her a binder for before it was finished; got involved in a dozen projects helping others, all the time growing more and more ill.

A doctor in Houston, Dr. Jack Rose, who was working on a new treatment for Hodgkin's Disease, took her as a patient. There would be periods of remission, then the Hodgkin's Disease would come back more fiercely than ever.

Sometimes the pain would be unbearable. Medication caused great hives. Once in pain she tried to get out of bed at a hospital, fell and fractured her skull. The tumors distorted her face, her neck was swollen almost to grotesqueness.

Once I came to the hospital room and she was looking at herself in the mirror. "Man, I'm a mess," she said. The last year she was in the hospital more often than she was at home. Josefa Guerra, who had been our neighbor in San Miguel, came to Austin to take care of the children.

Yet Barbara never really was a patient. When she

was well enough to do it she was out in the halls, visiting other people. In Houston, where many Hodgkin's Disease patients had come for treatment by Dr. Rose, they called her their cheer leader. She came to know each of the patients as friends and mourned when they died, as so many did, for they had come from many places in the country for one last chance and it was often too late.

She never complained but once I heard her almost complain. It was in the middle of the night. We slept in different rooms because she said I had to get my rest and I'd never get it the way she was turning and tossing.

Her voice woke me up. She was speaking earnestly, as if the one to whom she was talking was in the room with her.

"Listen," she said. "I know You never give anyone a cross heavier than they can carry. I know that all right and I believe it. But I'll tell you right now your idea of what I can bear is a whole lot more than I think I can."

She came to death in a wonderful way. In the last weeks all of the disfiguration disappeared. There were no more swellings. Her neck became as it was before she was ill. Her face was as it was. There was even less pain.

"What do you know," she said one day looking into a hand mirror. "I'm pretty again." And she was.

She liked to talk to people and many came to her room. Priests and sisters came and they talked long hours. A young priest friend of ours from his seminary days, Father Joseph Francis, who is now auxiliary bishop of Newark, stayed talking with her for more than an hour the last Sunday of her life.

There was one dreadful night, when seemingly unaware that she was speaking, she talked on and on. She talked of saints—described them—then she wept. Poor Martin Luther, she said, he didn't mean it to come out the way it did. She was a great admirer of John Kennedy, who a few months before had become president and she started weeping again. The poor young president, she said over and over again. Then her face tightened and she screamed—a scream like none I had ever heard before, a scream that sent shivers of fright through the Sister and me as we stood beside her bed. Hell is such a terrible place, such a terrible place, she said. And then her face changed, there was calm and joy in it. Heaven is such a wonderful place, so wonderful, so wonderful.

She remembered nothing of it the next day and until now I have never said anything to anyone about it.

She knew the day she was dying. She explained it to me. "I don't really feel bad. It is just that my legs are so hard and so cold, like they are turning to stone."

Father Emeric Lawrence, the Benedictine priest who was one of our cloest friends and the priest who witnessed our marriage, was in France and he had written her a letter about dying. Unaccountably, it had been delayed in the mail for more than two months and arrived only that day. It was a letter that was meant to help her face death and it was beautiful. I read it to her and she smiled. "Isn't that just like

Father Emeric to come to help me die," she said. She had me read it over and over to her.

A great many people came by and as soon as they came she would have them join her in prayers for the dying. Msgr. Maurice Deason, our pastor, came into the room often and each time he entered she smiled and said, "Let's get at that old litany again, Father."

She had made all her plans. She had many instructions for me. First of all, she said, you've got to start dressing better. She was never pleased that I wore jeans and had to be forced to wear a tie and coat.

She was stern about it. "I mean it, Dale. You have a position in life. Most of the time you dress like a bum. I want you to start dressing better."

She had chosen the undertaker, too. "I want to be buried from the funeral home for Mexican-Americans," she said. "I don't want to be buried at some fancy Anglo funeral home. When people come to my wake I want them to come to the Mexican part of town."

And she had other directions, too. She gave them to the Sisters. "When I die I don't want them to take my body out until there's nobody in the halls. That would just make people sad and I don't want people to be sad."

There was a constant stream of visitors to her room and she greeted them all and had them pray with her. It was about seven o'clock when she said to me, "You haven't had anything to eat all day. I want you to go out and get yourself something to eat."

I said Sister would bring me something from the

kitchen. She shook her head. "I want you to go out, Dale. I want you to go some place and get yourself a hamburger and a milk shake. I'll be all right. I want you to go out, Dale."

So I went. They said it was only a few minutes after I left that she hemorrhaged terribly and went into unconsciousness. I returned a half hour later and she was gone.

I went home. Josefa and Marianne were waiting for me. "She died," I said. Josefa began weeping. Marianne looked at me unbelieving. "Es no verdad," she said, "es no verdad, es no verdad." And she never spoke Spanish again.

Guy, our brain-injured son, was asleep and I didn't tell him until morning. He tried to understand, looked puzzled and then asked, "Mommy with Jesus?" I said, "Yes, Mommy's with Jesus." He clapped his hands in joy, "Mommy's with Jesus, Mommy's with Jesus." Then suddenly he stopped.

He looked at me, startled by the understanding. "I don't want Mommy with Jesus. I want Mommy with me. I don't want Mommy with Jesus, I want Mommy with me."

And he wept, all of us together wept. For me the weeping would not stop. Barbara had said she didn't want sadness when she died but that couldn't stop the sadness. It was Marianne who stopped my tears. I was weeping alone and she came to me.

"Daddy, shouldn't we be happy that Mommy has gone to Heaven?"

I said we should be.

"I don't think Mommy would want you to cry."

So I stopped my weeping.

The funeral Mass was on the Feast of Corpus Christi. Barbara would have wanted that. Whether it was liturgically proper or not, I do not know, but for her funeral Mass Msgr. Deason celebrated the Mass for the Feast of Corpus Christi and, although at the time it was not usual, everyone in the church, crowded to the walls, received Holy Communion. She had said she wanted that.

A strange thing happened the morning just before Barbara's funeral Mass. I'd found an old brown suit in my closet. I'd had it a long time but hardly ever wore it. But I remembered what she had told me about dressing right and I wore it. I was at the church when I noticed I was wearing old black shoes. I hadn't thought of that at all and didn't even have any brown shoes. But it wasn't right, wearing black shoes and a brown suit.

And suddenly there was something I knew, how, I have no idea at all.

I went to the rectory and Msgr. Deason's mother answered the bell.

"Mrs. Deason," I said. "I need some brown shoes to go with my suit. You have some brown shoes that I can wear."

"I'm sorry, Dale," she said. "Father doesn't have any brown shoes at all."

"I know where they are, Mrs. Deason," I said although I had no idea of why I was saying it. "They're around in a back hallway. Near the back door."

"Well, if you know where they are just come on in and get them," she said.

They were exactly where I knew they were. They were shiny new shoes and they fit me exactly. I put them on.

So I went to Mass looking like the gentleman Barbara had told me I should. My mind was too much occupied with other things to even think about it but when the Mass was over and Barbara's body was placed in a grave in the quiet cemetery where four years before she had said she would be buried, the wonder of it struck me.

I asked Father Deason about it. For awhile he couldn't think what I was talking about. Then he said, "That's strange. Just before I was going over for Mass there was a man at the back door. I didn't know who he was. He handed me the shoes, said he didn't need them any more and somebody would be needing them. I just put them down on the floor near the door and went to the church. I hadn't even thought about it until now."

But I had needed those brown shoes; I had known where they were.

I could hear Barbara laughing, "Now don't that beat all."

CHAPTER 32
The Second Time Around

When you are left in the world without your husband or wife, how do you take up your life again?

One reader, widowed but still comparatively young, wrote to me to say she had considered remarriage but she felt somehow that to do this would be untrue to her dead husband.

That is understandable. We don't stop loving those we have loved when they die, and it is difficult to readjust our thinking to the understanding of a new meaning of fidelity to that love.

The time to be true to the one you love is while you both are living. When there is death and one of the partners is left alone then the fidelity that is demanded is to life itself.

We must while we live make of our life something that has meaning. We must live as joyfully and usefully as we can. The infidelity would be to reject life, to no longer live joyfully and usefully in the present under the mistaken idea that we are bound in the past, not alone to our own lives but to the lives of those we loved who are gone.

When your life has been so completely intertwined with the life of another, life without that other seems unreal. It is a difficult thing to get into your mind that you are alive and that you must live alone.

When Barbara died I was left in a kind of confusion. I wanted to leave Austin, I wanted to start life again without the jabs of memory at the sight of familiar places. That, I think, is not a very practical solution for most people. It was for me. I had passed on the ownership of the diocesan paper to the diocese months before. There was nothing for me to do in Austin and had Barbara lived we would have sought out some other challenge.

But if I didn't know what I was going to do, one thing I knew for certain was that I would never marry again. Our marriage had been an extraordinarily good marriage. The very fact it had been such a good marriage was one of the reasons I did not want marriage again. I knew how many marriages there are that are not good. I'd had a wonderful marriage and I was satisfied with that.

Most of all, though, I didn't want to risk loving someone. There was great joy in our marriage but there was so much pain. It becomes almost unbearable when someone you love suffers. During seven years of illness there was great happiness but there was agony, too, the kind of agony you do not dare show the one you love. I could not risk loving again. I would never marry again. Of this I was certain. A year later I had married again.

Barbara talked to me about many things, told me things she wanted me to do, left me a great many directions. She had never talked to me about the question of my remarriage at any time. The question had never even occurred to me while she lived; it was just something I would never have thought about.

But Barbara had thought about it. She must have

known it was something impossible to talk to me
about. She was right about that. I wouldn't have allowed her to talk about it. But she thought about it
and she had directions for me.

She didn't take any chances her directions would
not be passed on to me. A month after her death, four
friends came to me with the same message. She had
told them there was something she wanted them to tell
me; a month after her death they were to give me the
message, no sooner, no later.

She must have thought there was a chance her
directions might not be passed on so she made certain
by giving the same message to four people.

What she said was that she wanted me to marry
again. One of the messages sounded like her. "You
know you can't take care of Marianne and Guy by
yourself. Josefa has a right to her own life so you can't
depend on her. You not only couldn't comb Marianne's hair, you wouldn't even know if it was combed.
Find yourself a good wife and keep on living."

I couldn't accept the message she left for me.
Barbara didn't understand. It just wasn't right for me.

It was Marianne who convinced me, trying to comfort me. She was ten, a compassionate child. I was
sitting quietly one evening, thinking about the many
things that were ahead of me.

"Don't you worry, Dad," she said. "I'll stay with
you and I will take care of you as long as you live."

Oh, no, she wouldn't. I'd known a woman who had
taken care of her widowed father. She had been about
Marianne's age when her mother died and she built

her whole life around her father. When she did finally marry, her husband was never first in her heart. Even when her father had died, she remained daddy's little girl.

That wasn't going to happen to Marianne. I hugged her and said, "That's nice, Marianne." But then it was I decided I was going to marry again.

But the whole idea overwhelmed me. I wasn't, at 44, going to get into the dating game, it's too much like roulette. I thought of widows I knew, of women who were unmarried. There was just no one.

Guy had gone to summer camp with the Carmelite Sisters of St. Therese of the Infant Jesus at Oklahoma City. Their Holy Child School seemed the place for him. He had a special happiness being with children handicapped as he was, no longer in competition with normal children. When I left him there he had laughed saying goodbye, traced a cross on my forehead (the way we said goodbye to each other) and run off to play without even looking back.

I'd found a job. Charlie Bennett at the *Daily Oklahoman* had offered me a job, writing editorials for *The Times,* the afternoon paper. I hadn't said I would accept. I try to make decisions on feast days of Our Lady, so I told him I'd come on August 15th to give my final answer. I'd already decided, though. I wanted to get back to daily newspaper work, where I had started.

I wanted to take a long trip back East before that, first of all, to visit Barbara's mother in North Carolina, then back to Ohio to visit with my two sisters and finally to Indiana to stop by at *Our Sunday Visitor* offices. I wanted to continue our Operation Understanding edition for clergymen of other churches.

It was when I got to Indiana that I thought of Margaret. She had been our friend in the Notre Dame years. She had worked for me in the publications office and she was the best secretary I ever had.

Barbara liked her and had her come to our home, once in hope she might start a romance between a student friend of ours and Margaret. It didn't work out, our friend said Margaret was too popular. He didn't want that kind of competition.

If things went well in the work I did at Notre Dame—and it did—it was mostly because of Margaret who seemed to anticipate what I wanted done and often did it before I even asked.

When she was twenty-one we gave her a statue of the Blessed Virgin—to start your home some day, Barbara said.

Margaret left when she became engaged and started preparing for a wedding sometime a year away and we missed her. It was at the time we were going to North Carolina. We heard later she had decided not to marry and had returned to Notre Dame.

There were probably Christmas cards between us, I'm not certain. Once when things at The Sign of the Cross were becoming complicated by my inability to keep up with accounts and correspondence, Barbara said we should ask Margaret if she would come to help us, but I rejected the idea: "Margaret should get married and you know there aren't many eligible young Catholic men here." Barbara agreed but added, "It would be good to have her. She takes such good care of you."

It was nearly ten years before we heard anything about Margaret again. Her uncle, Larry Baldinger, was head of the science school at Notre Dame, and he came on a speaking assignment to Texas and stopped by to visit us. We asked about Margaret. She was in Fort Wayne, he said, the secretary to the president of Lincoln Life. She had never married and I said I didn't understand that. If ever I'd known anyone who should have been a wife and mother it was Margaret. It just didn't seem to me possible she'd still not be married. "Maybe God has other plans for her," Barbara said.

It was strange I had not thought of Margaret but it was not until I was at *Our Sunday Visitor* that I remembered she was at Fort Wayne.

I phoned Lincoln Life, they rang her office, someone else answered, "Miss Alexander is away from her desk . . .," she began. "Oh, here she is now."

We exchanged greetings, she told me how sorry she was about Barbara. I asked her if she would go to dinner with me. She said her sister and her family were in town, they were going to eat at her home and she invited me to come.

I was at her home for three hours. She seemed just as she had always been; we talked easily. We were never alone during the entire evening but it was as if there hadn't been a decade between the time we'd last seen each other and now.

The next day Marianne and I started back for

Texas. Margaret and I began corresponding. Before I returned north in the fall, we had already decided by letter that we would marry.

I went to Oklahoma City on August 15th. After Mass I went down to the newspaper office. I was looking forward to the work. We sat down to talk. "Have you decided to come with us?" Charlie asked.

"No, I haven't," I said, hardly believing I was saying it. "Oh," he said in surprise. He wasn't as surprised as I was. "What are you going to do?" he asked. "I'm going back to my home town, Troy, Ohio. I have to start my life again, I want to start it where I started it before." That was an answer that surprised me, too, I'd never thought of it before.

So a few months later I headed back for my home town, became editor of the daily paper where I'd started as a newspaperman thirty years before as a kid of fourteen.

The next year Margaret and I were married at St. John the Baptist Church in Fort Wayne. So Guy and Marianne had a mother again; Marianne had someone to comb her hair. When we were ready to leave the altar we went to the Blessed Virgin's altar and prayed that we would have children. Two years later Rita Kathryn was born.

I have been twice blessed in my life. Some men are not blessed with even one good wife, I've been blessed by two of the most wonderful women who ever have lived on God's good earth.

CHAPTER 33

A Sacrament That Is Always

"I want my marriage to be a good marriage. I've seen too many marriages that failed. It happened with my own parents and they were good Catholics. Is there something we should know, something we should do, to help make our marriage a good marriage?"

It seems to me the beginning of understanding in a Catholic marriage is in realizing that marriage is a Sacrament and not just a Sacrament received once but a Sacrament that can be received continuously.

Sometimes in speaking to married couples I begin by asking how many of those present received the grace of the Sacrament of marriage within the last month. Sometimes a newly-married couple will raise their hands but usually not a hand is raised.

And that comes because of a misunderstanding, just as there is a common misunderstanding about how the Sacrament is administered. People say they were married by Father So-and-so but they weren't. The priest witnesses a marriage, he doesn't administer the Sacrament. The Sacrament is administered by the husband to the wife, the wife to the husband.

Nor does husband administer the Sacrament to his wife and the wife to the husband on only one special occasion. The Sacrament of marriage is a continuing Sacrament; the graces that come to us we are constantly offering each other.

Every act of love between us brings the grace of the

Sacrament to us. I am not speaking just of the physical act of conjugal love, although I am including it, but of every act that derives from the love a husband has for his wife, the wife has for her husband.

The husband brings grace to the marriage when he opens the door of the car for his wife because he loves her. The wife brings grace to the marriage when she prepares her husband's favorite dish. Whatever husband and wife do for each other because they love each other brings the working of grace in the marriage.

Whatever we might do in anger, whatever we might do that hurts the other, whatever we do that does not offer love, can impede the flow of grace. But the happy remedy to this is in our love for each other.

In marriage we are spiritually one and we have as our greatest responsibility to each other the eternal salvation of both of us. And we are given a continuing Sacrament to not only assure us of this but to bring us happiness through all our lives.

That so few married people understand the way in which they can bring a continuing flow of grace in their marriage is why so few take conscious advantage of this great gift.

When I say that we bring grace to each other, it is important to understand I am not talking just about the things we do that are of a spiritual nature. It is good that we go to Mass together, that we pray together, that we see in each other the love of God we possess. We do receive graces through these things.

But the grace that comes to us through the Sacrament of marriage comes through the ordinary things we do. The kindnesses we show one another, the little things we do out of our love, even the tolerance we show for the faults we have bring the working of grace into our marriage.

We do not come to marriage alone, just the two of us. God is with us and His graces we make operative in our marriage by our own acts of love.

It is important to understand marriage as a continuing Sacrament but for a marriage to be successful there are things we must do on a human level.

We are told the husband is the head of the family. Sometimes husbands insist on this to the detriment of happiness in the marriage. It must not be understood as an authoritarian role. I'm not even certain how it is to be understood but what I do know is that husbands must not only love but respect their wives, and wives must not only love but respect their husbands, and each must want for the other that which is best for the other, always.

That is the key, that each wants what is best for the other. The man in marriage, the woman in marriage, can never seek advantage for self but out of love want what is of advantage to the other. It has been said marriage is a fifty-fifty proposition. I think it cannot be; the happy marriage is the one in which each partner offers to the other 100 percent of self.

But in another sense there must be sharing. In a sense there is a sharing in the very fact each is seeking what is best for the other. But on a human level there must be another kind of sharing.

Husbands and wives must communicate with each

other. The husband who sets his work aside apart from his marriage does not really share himself fully with his wife. The wife who has a social life that she thinks of no interest to her husband and so something she does not discuss at all with him, fails to share herself with her husband.

CHAPTER 34
Marriage Is Sharing

"We have been married less than a year. Already there are signs in our marriage of problems. Instead of becoming closer to each other we are drifting further apart."

Husbands and wives must share their whole lives with each other. I've known husbands who think their wives wouldn't be interested in their work, who come home wanting to get away from the work they've been doing all day, who simply never talk to their wives at all about what is a major part of their lives.

But there must be a sharing of the whole life. If spiritually we are one, then we should be one in fact. There should not be a schizophrenia in marriage in which husbands keep part of their lives away from their wives and wives keep part of their lives away from husbands.

So talking to each other is important. But, because there is a difference, it is important to understand that we must not only talk to each other, we must listen to each other.

There are problems that every marriage faces, problems about the way in which the income is to be used, problems relating to careers, decisions to be made concerning children. In all of these it is necessary that husbands and wives talk to each other and listen to each other.

Decisions that are made should be reached in

mutual harmony. The reaching of decisions should be made in love, not as adversaries seeking to hammer out some compromise, but in love by caring persons wanting what is best for each and both.

Just as we would not knowingly or willingly do harm to ourselves, cause ourselves pain, we should devote ourselves to making certain we never do harm or bring pain to the one with whom we are united in marriage.

It is a sadness but in some marriages people do hurt each other—do it knowingly. A wife discovers the husband is sensitive about the receding hairline or the husband learns the wife is sensitive about the dress size she has outgrown. Then in a dispute one takes advantage of the other's sensitive point. This is not just cruel, not just destructive; it is a perversion.

Husbands and wives must from the very beginning commit themselves to not bring pain to each other. We must, if we have fallen into this perversion, eradicate it.

Because all of us have our weaknesses, make mistakes, unknowingly may bring pain to the other, then our love for each other must be great enough to accept the faults of the other. But that doesn't really say it. Simply accepting the faults of the other is not enough. What is needed is something more than just acceptance; what is necessary is an embracing of the one we love as he or she is. Then there is no need for acceptance because we love each other as we are, with all our faults.

Many of the letters I receive come from wives whose husbands have abandoned them for another woman, or from men whose wives have abandoned them for another man.

Sometimes I've talked with those who have abandoned their commitment to marriage for another person. The most common explanation I've heard is that it just happened, that the one who left wife or husband, just fell in love with someone else.

That may be a necessary rationalization but it is nonsense and those who offer it know it is nonsense. Husbands don't leave wives and wives don't leave husbands without doing it through conscious steps. It may well be they are in eventual situations in which passions take control but they move to those situations by avoidable steps.

Our modern society takes such a casual attitude towards extra-marital intimacies and towards divorce that the mores of this society almost encourage infidelity. But those who are united in Christian marriage cannot help but know that the casual attitude towards marriage is wrong.

The fidelity a man and a woman owe to each other in Christian marriage is in the wholeness of their relationship to each other. It comes in the whole sharing of self with the other; it comes in always seeking what is best for the other; it comes in living for the other.

It astonishes me when I'm told some husbands never tell their wives they love them and some wives never tell their husbands they love them.

I'm not sure why it is but some people do have difficulty in telling those they love that they love them.

Whatever it is, it is wrong and harmful. Never let a day pass that you do not tell those that you love that you love them.

I gave this advice once to a woman who told me that she and her husband never spoke of their love. "If I started telling him now that I love him, he'd wonder what was the matter," she said. That may be but you can't wait until tomorrow to do what you should do today because one thing we are certain to run out of is tomorrows.

The success of Marriage Encounter has come because it asks husbands and wives to do what they should have been doing all along, sharing thoughts with each other, letting the other know things that bother, and especially in expressing love through words and actions.

That's what marriage is about. Those who are just getting married must start this way from the beginning. Those who have failed in this sharing, in this expression of love, must do now what they've failed to do in the past.

CHAPTER 35
A Final Word About Caring

The dictionary tells us that caring is the present participle of the intransitive verb care, which means to show concern.

In the Christian sense, caring means concern for all things and all people.

We do not live in isolation. We live among other people. To attempt to live without caring is not to really live at all. Living is caring.

Caring does not mean being unconcerned about our own selves. We must have concern for ourselves; this is a part of caring. But caring means we cannot stop with concern about our own selves; we must reach out to all people.

If we are caring this does not mean all our problems are solved. In a sense, if we care enough our problems are increased because our concern is for all people and their problems become our own.

But it is only by reaching out to others that we really live. People need people, the popular song goes, and it is the truth. We need people and people need us.

There is no magic formula for living a caring life. We all of us are struggling people, trying to do the best we can. You will have found in this book no certain formula for living; it has not been intended that you should.

But because we are people living together there is value in sharing with each other the experiences we have in life. Experiences are not interchangeable—our situations are always unique—but in the sharing of experiences it is possible to find in another's life hints of explanations.

Let us care about one another.